To
Eileen,

WALKING CALIFORNIA'S DESERT PARKS

All Best &
Happy Desert Trails,
John McKinney

Also by John McKinney

A Walk Along Land's End

Other books in the *Walking the West* Series:

Walking California's Central Coast

Walking California's State Parks

Walking the California Coast

Walking Los Angeles

Walking Southern California

Walking the East Mojave

Walking Santa Barbara

Walking California's Desert Parks

A Day Hiker's Guide

John McKinney

HarperSanFrancisco

An Imprint of HarperCollins*Publishers*

▨ A TREE CLAUSE BOOK

HarperSanFrancisco and the author, in association with The Basic Foundation, a not-for-profit-organization whose primary mission is reforestation, will facilitate the planting of two trees for every one tree used in the manufacture of this book.

Portions of this book have appeared in the author's hiking column in the *Los Angeles Times*.

HarperCollins Web Site: http://www.harpercollins.com

HarperCollins®, ▨®, HarperSanFrancisco™, and A TREE CLAUSE BOOK® are trademarks of HarperCollins Publishers, Inc.

Maps designed by Susan Kuromiya

FIRST EDITION

Library of Congress Cataloging-in-Publication Data:

McKinney, John.

    Walking California's desert parks : a day hiker's guide / John McKinney. — 1st ed.

Includes index.

ISBN 0–06–258637–8 (pbk.)

1. Hiking—California—Guidebooks. 2. Deserts—California—Guidebooks. 3. Parks—California—Guidebooks. 4. California—Guidebooks. I. Title. II. Series.

GV199.42.C2M357 1996

796.5'1'09794—dc20   95–51517

96 97 98 99 00 ❖ RRD(H) 10 9 8 7 6 5 4 3 2 1

Contents

California's Desert Parks

The desert is the opposite of all that we naturally find pleasing. Yet I believe that its hold upon those who have once fallen under its spell is deeper and more enduring than is the charm of forest or sea or mountain.

—*Joseph Chase*, California Desert Trails

Many travelers drive along California's coast or through the state's forests and feel inspired by the scenery. A drive through the desert, however, rarely provides similar inspiration. Too flat, too barren, unaccommodating is the opinion of many motorists.

The desert demands a closer look. To appreciate fully the desert's beauty requires a bit of walking—a stroll on a nature trail looping around a park campground, a hike to a palm oasis, a trek to the top of a desert peak. Without a doubt, the desert is most seductive when approached on foot.

The desert, first in the hearts of the many who love it, was the last of the state's regions to be preserved. Early conservationists first worked to preserve the glorious mountains and forests; next came the coast and coastal mountains. And finally, the desert.

The desert's recreation potential followed a similar pattern. First Californians took to the mountains, then to the seashore, lastly to the desert. At the beginning of the twentieth century, resorts and recreation of all sorts were well established in the state's alpine and coastal regions, but only a few hardy prospectors roamed the desert.

It wasn't until the 1920s and the development of (somewhat) dependable autos that Americans began discovering the desert. During that decade, there was a worldwide fascination with the desert, and cactus gardens were very much in vogue. Entrepreneurs hauled truckloads of desert plants into Los Angeles for quick sale or export. The Mojave was being picked clean of its cacti, yucca, and ocotillo. A wealthy Pasadena socialite, Minerva Hoyt, organized the International Desert Conservation League to halt this destructive practice. Through her lobbying efforts and crusade in Washington, D.C., Joshua Tree National Monument was established in 1936.

In one of his last official acts, President Herbert Hoover signed a proclamation designating Death Valley as a national monument on

February 11, 1933. With the stroke of a pen he not only legislated the protection of a vast and wondrous land, but also helped to transform one of the earth's least hospitable spots into a popular tourist destination.

Over the years, public attitudes about the desert completely changed. Land that had previously been considered hideously devoid of life was now celebrated for its spare beauty; places that had once been feared for their harshness were now admired for their uniqueness. Today the desert's desolation seems to attract rather than repel visitors.

In October 1994, Congress passed the landmark California Desert Protection Act, which created the 1.4-million-acre Mojave National Preserve. It also expanded Joshua Tree National Monument and Death Valley National Monument and "upgraded" them to national parks. Further, the desert act designated another 3.5 million acres of land in sixty-nine different areas as wilderness to be managed by the U.S. Bureau of Land Management.

In signing the bill, President Clinton proclaimed: "The broad vistas, the rugged mountain ranges, and the evidence of the human past are treasures that merit protection on behalf of the American people."

California visitors are fortunate in having not one, but two vast deserts to explore: the Mojave and the Colorado. The Mojave is referred to as a high desert, for reasons of latitude and altitude. There is (relatively) more rainfall in this region, and the hot season is not as hot and severe as it is in the lower desert.

The Colorado Desert, in the extreme southeastern portion of California, is only a small part of the larger Sonoran Desert, which covers 120,000 square miles of the American Southwest. Lower in elevation than the Mojave Desert, it is therefore hotter and drier.

Death Valley National Park. A park? The forty-niners whose suffering gave the valley its name would have howled at the notion. With passage of the California Desert Protection Act of 1994, Death Valley became the largest national park outside Alaska with more than 3.3 million acres.

One place to take in the enormity of the park is from the crest of the Black Mountains at Dante's View or Coffin Peak. A never-to-be-forgotten panorama unfolds. A vertical mile down lies the lowest spot on the continent. Opposite the overlooks, across the valley, rise Telescope Peak and snow-clad summits of the Panamints. Farther still, on the western horizon, loom the granite ramparts of the Sierra Nevada. North and south from Dante's View rise the Funeral Mountains. And from here, too, you can see the glimmer of that alkaline pool known as Badwater—or is it just a mirage?

Mountains stand naked, unadorned; the bitter waters of saline lakes evaporate into bizarre, razor-sharp crystal formations; jagged canyons jab deep into the earth. Ovenlike heat, frigid cold, and the driest air imaginable combine to make this one of the most inhospitable locations in the world.

Badwater, the lowest point in the Western Hemisphere at 282 feet below sea level, is also one of the hottest places in the world, with regularly recorded summer temperatures of 120°F.

Many of Death Valley's topographical features are associated with hellish images—Funeral Mountains, Furnace Creek, Dante's View, Coffin Peak, and Devil's Golf Course—but the national park can be a place of great serenity.

Southwest of Death Valley National Park is a region known loosely as the West Mojave. The West presents great sandscapes, with many flat areas and some isolated ridges and buttes. Some of the strange geology includes the otherworldly Trona Pinnacles, backdrop for a *Star Trek* movie, and the Devil's Punchbowl, a bizarre earthquake-fractured basin.

Situated south of the Tehachapi Mountains and northwest of the San Gabriel Mountains, the Antelope Valley makes up the western frontier of the Mojave Desert. Natural attractions include a reserve for the state's official flower—the California poppy—and another reserve for the endangered desert tortoise.

Just a few hours' drive from Los Angeles is a virtually undiscovered gem of the desert, sometimes referred to as the East Mojave Desert or as "The Lonesome Triangle." Within the triangle bounded by Interstate 15 on the north and Interstate 40 to the south, Barstow on the west and Needles on the east, is Mojave National Preserve. It is a land of great diversity—of grand mesas and a dozen mountain ranges, of sand dunes and extinct volcanoes.

The view from the busy highway on the way to Las Vegas offers few hints of the unique desert environment beyond: cinder cones, dry lake beds, tabletop mesas. Beckoning the hiker are the magnificent 700-foot Kelso Dunes, along with the world's largest Joshua tree forest.

In places, the Colorado Desert appears too civilized. Extensive irrigation for agriculture and a host of water reclamation projects give it an unnatural green. In Palm Springs, imported water, land speculators, and eager developers have created a renowned resort area in what was once considered the middle of nowhere.

Before the 1930s, Palm Springs had successively been the domain of Cahuilla Indians, a stagecoach stop, and a healing place for the convalescent and the tubercular. When a paved road linked Palm

Springs to Los Angeles, actors and directors began wintering in the desert. Sixty years of growth have brought enormous changes to the resort, but it remains the most popular and widely known desert recreation center in the world.

The hills and canyons bordering Palm Springs have the greatest concentration of palm trees in North America, and Palm Canyon just south of the city in the Agua Caliente Indian Reservation has more trees than any other desert oasis. A meandering stream and lush undergrowth complement more than 3,000 palms, creating a junglelike atmosphere in some places. Tree lovers enjoy the California fan palms, some of them estimated to be 2,000 years old.

Located just east of Palm Springs is Joshua Tree National Park. Well known for its incredible granite boulders that attract rock climbers and for its forest of Joshua trees, the reserve lures visitors as a year-round destination for many outdoor activities, particularly hiking and camping.

The Joshua tree is said to have been named by early Mormon settlers traveling west. The trees' upraised limbs and bearded appearance reminded them of the prophet Joshua leading them to the promised land. Despite its harsh appearance, the tree belongs to the lily family.

One of the many fascinations of the national park is the Wonderland of Rocks, 12 square miles of massive, jumbled granite. This curious maze of stone hides groves of Joshua trees, trackless washes, and several small pools of water.

California's largest state park, with 763 square miles, is Anza-Borrego Desert State Park, named for the Mexican explorer Juan Bautista de Anza and a bighorn sheep. De Anza traveled through the region in 1774, and the sheep still roam some parts of the park. This diverse desert park boasts more than 20 palm groves and year-round creeks, great stands of cholla and elephant trees, slot canyons, and badland formations. Numerous trails explore the park.

The California desert includes not only the 3 huge parks under National Park Service stewardship and vast Anza-Borrego under state parks administration, but millions of acres in the care of the U.S. Bureau of Land Management. Dozens of BLM locales are now managed as wilderness areas and offer breathtaking adventure way off the tourist track.

Acknowledgments

The author would like to express his sincere appreciation for the expertise offered during the preparation of this guide by the National Park Service, the California Department of Parks and Recreation, and the U.S. Bureau of Land Management. A special thank you goes to the rangers, superintendents, and office and field personnel who care for the California desert, and who so courteously field- and fact-checked the information in this guide.

Walking California's Desert Parks

California's desert parks and preserves are grouped by geography into chapters, then further organized in rough north-to-south order. Most of the hiking locales clearly belong in their respective categories, but I've made judgment calls on where to place a couple of parks that straddle geographical areas. For example, Darwin Falls is in the West Mojave Desert and until recently was under the jurisdiction of the U.S. Bureau of Land Management. Now, however, it's part of Death Valley National Park, so I "transferred" Darwin Falls to the Death Valley chapter. Agua Caliente County Park is an island of San Diego County Parks Department land in the midst of vast Anza-Borrego Desert State Park, so I included this hot springs and hike in the Anza-Borrego Desert State Park chapter. Well, you get the idea.

For each destination, I briefly mention **Terrain** and **Highlights,** followed by **Distance,** expressed in round-trip mileage figures. The hikes in this guide range from 1 to 15 miles, with the majority in the 5- to 8-mile range. Gain or loss in elevation follows the mileage.

Degree of Difficulty is provided to help you match a walk to your ability. You'll want to consider both mileage and elevation as well as condition of the trail, terrain, and season. Remember to take a more conservative approach to walking in the desert than you might with more forgiving terrain. Hot sands, exposed chaparral, or miles of boulder-hopping can make a short walk seem long.

Hikers vary a great deal in relative physical condition, but you may want to consider the following: An easy walk suitable for beginners and children would be less than 5 miles with an elevation gain of less than 700 or 800 feet. A moderate walk is one in the 5- to 10-mile range, with under 2,000 feet of elevation gain. You should be reasonably fit for these. Preteens sometimes find the going difficult. Hikes of more than 10 miles and those with more than a 2,000-foot gain are for experienced hikers in top form.

Season is the next item to consider. Most of the walks in this book are best done in autumn, winter, or spring. With the exception of a couple of high mountain regions—Telescope Peak above Death Valley, the White Mountains, Mount San Jacinto—summer hiking in the desert is far too uncomfortable and dangerous to consider.

Precautions have been noted in some cases. While the desert receives very little rain, when it does fall dangerous flood conditions often result. A few trails in this guide may be impassable in winter and spring because of high water. Relevant flood information has been included in the text.

An introduction to each walk describes what you'll see in a particular park, preserve, or wilderness area, and what you'll observe along the trail: plants, animals, panoramic views. You'll also learn about the geologic and human history of the region.

The **Directions to trailhead** take you from the nearest major highway to trailhead parking. For trails having two desirable trailheads, directions to each are given. A few trails can be walked one way, with the possibility of a car shuttle. Suggested car-shuttle points are noted.

After the directions to the trailhead, you'll read a description of **The walk.** Important junctions and major sights are pointed out, but I've left for you to discover the multitude of little things that make a hike an adventure.

Options allow you to climb higher or farther or take a different route back to the trailhead.

On the Trail

Choose the pace that's best for you. Rest once an hour for a few minutes. To keep your momentum and to avoid stiffness, it's better to take several short rests rather than one long one. Set a steady pace, one you can keep up all day. Wear a watch, not because you have an appointment with a palm oasis and must be punctual, but because a watch gives you some idea of pace and helps you get back to the trailhead before dark.

Walking uphill takes energy. Walking 2 miles an hour up a 10 percent grade requires as much energy as hiking 4 miles an hour on level trail. Climbing can be especially difficult at high altitudes.

Many people prefer walking solo, but having two or three in your party is a definite advantage: If something goes wrong, someone can go for help. Hiking with a group is a good idea for first-time walkers.

Alas, backcountry travelers are not always immune from urban attitudes, stresses, and crimes. While most of our state and national parks are far safer than our urban environment, walkers—particularly women walkers—must be aware that unsavory characters are not unknown on the trail. Your "street smarts" coupled with your trail sense are two keys to avoiding trouble.

Sometimes, after a few hikes, a craving for solitude develops—by which time you should be able to take care of yourself on the trail. There's a lot to be said for solitary hiking, as the writings of Thoreau, Whitman, and Muir would seem to indicate.

Walking Hints

Many day hikes require little more equipment than comfortable shoes, yet hikers often overburden themselves with such nonessentials as hunting knives, hatchets, and propane stoves. The idea with equipment is to take only what you need. You want to get so comfortable with your equipment that you don't think about it; what little you need is on your back and what you don't need is far away.

Footwear: Day hiking begins and ends with the feet. If you're carrying a day pack over easy terrain you don't need a heavy pair of boots. Running shoes or walking shoes can even serve to get you started. But if you do much hiking over rough terrain, a good pair of boots is necessary and well worth the money. A lightweight pair with a Vibram sole will do nicely. Don't buy more boot than you need. A number of fine walking shoes and running shoe–hiking boot combinations on the market will give you miles of comfortable walking.

Blisters can ruin any hike, so be sure to break in your boots before you hit the trail. Walk around town until your feet develop a callous indifference to your boots.

Clothing: You probably have most of what you need in your closet.

A T-shirt layered with a button-down cotton shirt gives you lots of temperature-regulating possibilities. Add a wool shirt and a windbreaker with a hood and you'll be protected against sudden changes in temperatures.

Shorts are useful much of the year in the desert. Test your shorts by stepping up on a chair. If they pull around the groin, butt, or thigh, they're too tight.

For cooler days or walking through brush, a sturdy pair of long pants is necessary.

Hats prevent the brain from frying and protect from heat loss when it is cold.

Sunglasses are a must for desert hiking. Make sure you buy a pair that provides UV protection. Apply sunscreen to your face and other exposed skin.

Food: On a day hike, weight is no problem, so you can pack whatever you wish. Remember to pack out what you pack in. The day you hike is not the day to diet. There's a lot of calorie burning on a hike and quite an energy cost. You'll need all your strength, particularly on steep grades. Gorp, or trail mix, with dried fruit, nuts, raisins, and M&M's, is high-octane fuel. A sandwich, fruit, and cookies make a good lunch. Avoid a big lunch. Exertion after a big lunch sets up a competition between your stomach and your legs. Your legs lose, and you may develop weakness and indigestion.

Water: It's still possible to drink from some backcountry streams and springs without ill effect, but each such water source should be carefully scrutinized. I highly recommend that you avoid drinking untreated water in any desert park, preserve, or wilderness area.

Carry lots of water—2 quarts per person per day hike at a minimum. And be sure to drink it to stay hydrated!

First Aid Kit: Carry a standard kit supplemented with an Ace bandage in the event of hiker's knee or a sprained ankle. Take moleskin for blisters. Insect repellent won't stop mosquitoes from buzzing around but it will inhibit their biting.

Day Pack or "Summit Pack": A day pack is a soft, frameless pack that attaches to your shoulders and sometimes includes a hip band or waist belt for support. A good one will last a lifetime. Those thin cotton or nylon bike bags and book bags won't hold up well. Shoulder pads are a nice feature in a day pack. You'll only be carrying five or ten pounds, but the pads are comfortable on a long hike. Get a pack with a tough covered zipper. Double-O rings slip and aren't the greatest shoulder strap adjusters. Get tabler buckles; they don't slip and they adjust quickly.

Precautions

We still react instinctively when we feel threatened by some aspect of the natural world. Don't let the few biters, stingers, and hazards mentioned below make you apprehensive about going into the backcountry.

Blisters: There's nothing worse than walking on feet that burn like hot coals. To avoid blisters, make sure your boots fit properly. Keep pulling up your socks and see to it that they don't bunch up. Act quickly if you feel a blister developing. Cut a hole in moleskin a little larger than your red spot and stick it in place with the blister poking through the hole. The idea is to surround it so the boot can't get at it. (If you covered it you could irritate it further, and you'd have to peel the tape off the blister. Ouch!) Some hikers put a double layer of tissue paper over the blister and fasten the tissue in place with surgical tape. If you get a full-grown blister, pop it with a clean needle inserted under the edge, apply antiseptic, and put moleskin over the area.

Poison Oak: Fortunately, except in the lushest canyons, you won't see much of this irritant in the California desert. The leaves, which grow in clusters of three, are one to four inches long and glossy, as if waxed.

All parts of the plant at all times of the year contain poisonous sap that can severely blister skin and mucous membranes. Its sap is most toxic during spring and summer. In fall, poison oak is particularly conspicuous; its leaves turn to flaming crimson or orange. However, since its color change is more a response to heat and dryness than to season, its "fall color" can occur anytime in California. Leaves on some plants can be turning yellow or red while plants in most spots are putting out green leaves. In winter, poison oak is naked, its stalks blending into the dull hue of the forest.

Rattlesnakes: Sometimes rattlesnakes take to the trail to enjoy the sunshine, so keep an eye out. Despite the common fear of rattlers, few people see them, even in the desert, and rarely is anyone bitten. Only a small percentage of bites cause serious injury.

If you've been bitten, remain calm. Check to be sure you've actually been envenomized. Look for swelling around the wound within 5 minutes. If it doesn't swell, you've probably escaped and may not require hospital treatment. If swelling and other symptoms occur— numbness around the lips or hairline, a metallic taste in the mouth, or twitching facial muscles—it got you and you need immediate treatment.

Getting to a hospital emergency room is more important than any other first aid. Keep the site of the wounds as immobilized as possible and relax. Cutting-and-suction treatments are now medically out of vogue and advised only as a last resort if you're absolutely sure you can't get to a hospital within four hours.

Bees: More fatalities occur from allergic reaction to insect stings than from rattlesnake bites. People allergic to bee stings can get a desensitization shot and a specially equipped bee kit from an allergist.

Ticks: These insects are ¼ to ½ inch long and about the color of the ground, so they're hard to see. Ticks are usually picked up by brushing against low vegetation. When hiking in a tick area it's best to sit on rocks rather than fallen logs. Check your skin and clothing occasionally. You and your loved one can groom each other like monkeys at the zoo. If one is attached to the skin, it should be lifted off with a slow gentle pull. Before bathing, look for ticks on the body, particularly in the hair and pubic region.

Lyme disease, while rare in California, is the most common tick-carried disease. Symptoms usually include a red, ringlike rash on the skin where the tick attaches itself. The rash is often accompanied by flulike symptoms of headaches, chills and fever, fatigue, and aching muscles. If the disease goes untreated, second-stage symptoms are meningitis and abnormal heartbeat; third-stage symptoms (months or years later) can include arthritis. A blood test can determine if a person is infected. Antibiotics are a very effective treatment.

Getting Lost and Found

Even experienced hikers can get lost. Getting lost is usually the result of taking a "shortcut" off an established trail. The danger is magnified if you venture out alone or fail to tell anyone where you've gone and when you expect to return.

Try to avoid getting lost in the first place. Know your physical condition and don't overtax yourself. Check your boots and clothing. Be prepared for bad weather. Inquire about trail conditions. Allow plenty of time for your hike, and even more time for your return to the trailhead.

When you're on the trail, keep your eyes open. If you're hiking so fast that all you see is your boots, you're not attentive to passing terrain—its charms or its layout. STOP once in a while. Sniff wildflowers, splash your face in a spring. LISTEN. Maybe the trail is paralleling a stream. Listen to the sound of mountain water. On your left? On your right? LOOK AROUND. That's the best insurance against getting lost.

So you're really lost? Stay calm. Don't worry about food. It takes weeks to starve to death. Besides, you've got that candy bar in your day pack. You have a canteen. And you have a poncho in case of rain. You're in no immediate danger, so don't run around in circles like a mindless chicken.

LOOK AROUND some more. Are there any familiar landmarks in sight? Have you been gaining elevation or losing it? Where has the sun been shining? On your right cheek? Your back? Retrace your steps, if you can. Look for other footprints. If you're totally disoriented, keep walking laterally. Don't go deeper into that desert canyon. Go upslope to get a good view, but don't trek aimlessly here and there.

If it's near dark, get ready to spend the night. Don't try to find your way out in the dark. Don't worry. If you left your itinerary, your rescuers will begin looking for you in the morning. The universal distress call is three visible or audible signals: three shouts or whistles, three shiny objects placed on a bare summit. Don't build a fire! You could start a major conflagration.

Relax and think of your next hike. You'll make it, don't worry.

Backcountry Courtesy

Leave your radio and tape player at home.

Dogs must be kept on a leash at all times and enclosed in a vehicle or tent at night. Dogs are not allowed on many trails in parks and wilderness areas; regulations vary from area to area.

No smoking on trails.

Resist the urge to collect flowers, rocks, or animals. It disrupts nature's balance and lessens the wilderness experience for future hikers.

Litter detracts from even the most beautiful backcountry setting. If you packed it in, you can pack it out.

You have a moral obligation to help a hiker in need. Give whatever first aid or comfort you can, and then hurry for help.

Don't cut switchbacks.

Desert Survival Safety Rules

When planning a trip into the desert, always tell someone where you are going, when you expect to return, and what your route will be. Stick to your plan.

Carry at least one gallon of water per person per day of your trip. (Plastic gallon jugs are handy and portable.)

Be sure your vehicle is in good condition with a sound battery, good hoses, spare tire, spare fan belt, radiator water, necessary tools, and reserve gasoline and oil.

Keep an eye on the sky. Flash floods may occur in a wash any time thunderheads are in sight, even though it may not rain a drop where you're standing.

If caught in a dust storm while driving, get off the road. Turn off driving lights, turn on emergency flashers, and back into the wind to reduce windshield pitting by sand particles.

Before driving through washes and sandy areas, test the footing. One minute on foot may save hours of hard work or prevent a punctured oil pan.

If your vehicle breaks down, stay near it. Your emergency supplies are here. Your car has many other items useful in an emergency. Raise the hood and trunk lid to denote "help needed." A vehicle can be seen for miles, but a person on foot is very difficult to find.

When not moving, use available shade or make your own with tarps, blankets, seat covers—anything available to reduce the rays of the sun. Do not sit or lie directly on the ground, which may be 30° or more hotter than the air.

Leave a disabled vehicle only if you are positive of the route to help. Leave a note for rescuers that lists the time you left and the direction you are taking.

If you must walk, rest for at least 10 minutes out of each hour. If you are not normally physically active, rest up to 30 minutes out of each hour. Find shade, sit down, and prop up your feet. Adjust shoes and socks. Do not remove shoes; you may not be able to get them back on swollen feet.

If you have water, drink it. Do not ration it.

If water is limited, keep your mouth shut. Do not talk, do not eat, do not smoke, do not drink alcohol, do not take salt.

Keep clothing on; it helps keep the body temperature down and reduces the dehydration rate. Cover your head. If you don't have a hat, improvise a head covering.

A roadway is a sign of civilization. If you find a road, stay on it.

When hiking in the desert, equip each person, especially children, with a police-type whistle. It makes a distinctive noise with little effort. Three blasts denote "help needed."

To avoid poisonous creatures, put your hands or feet only where you can see them.

The following list comes from the manual *Desert Survival: Information for Anyone Traveling in the Desert Southwest*, published by the Maricopa County Department of Civil Defense and Emergency Services.

Emergency Equipment

First-aid kit

Fire extinguisher

Blanket

Shovel

Knife

Flashlight

Signal mirror

Road flares

Repair Items

Jack and lug wrench

Tire pump

Tow chain

Tow rope

Electrical tape

Duct tape

Baling wire

Tool kit

Commodities

Water (absolute minimum, one gallon per person per day)

Extra oil and gas

Toilet tissue

Weatherproof matches

Concentrated food

Personal Items

Compass

Map of area

Protective clothing

Sunglasses

Hat

Sunscreen

Pen and paper

Death Valley offers sights unique in all the world.

1. Death Valley National Park

Entering Death Valley National Park at Towne Pass, State Highway 190 crests the rolling Panamint Range and descends into Emigrant Wash. Along the road I spot the new sign: WELCOME TO DEATH VALLEY NATIONAL PARK.

Death Valley National Park? The forty-niners, whose suffering gave the valley its name, would have howled at the notion. Death Valley National Park seems a contradiction in terms, an oxymoron of the great outdoors.

Four-letter words other than *park* are more often associated with Death Valley: gold, mine, heat, lost, dead. And the four-letter words shouted by teamsters who drove the twenty-mule-team borax wagons need not be repeated.

There is something about the desert, and especially this desert, that at first glance seems the antithesis of all that park-goers find desirable. To the needs of most park visitors—shade, water, and easy-to-follow self-guided nature trails—Death Valley answers with a resounding no.

And the word *park* suggests a landscape under human control. In this great land of extremes, nothing could be further from the truth. A bighorn sheep standing watch atop painted cliffs, sunlight and shadow playing over the salt and soda floor, a blue-gray cascade of gravel pouring down a gorge to a land below the level of the sea—this territory is as ungovernable as are its flaming sunsets.

In Death Valley, the forces of the earth are exposed to view with dramatic clarity: a sudden fault and a sink became a lake; then the water evaporated, leaving behind borax and, above all, fantastic scenery. Although Death Valley is called a valley, in actuality it is not. Valleys are carved by rivers. Death Valley is what geologists call a graben. Here a block of the earth's crust has dropped down along fault lines below the surrounding mountain walls.

At Racetrack Playa, a dry lake bed, visitors puzzle over rocks that weigh as much as ¼ ton and move mysteriously across the mud floor, leaving trails as a record of their movement. Research suggests that a combination of powerful winds and rain may skid the rocks over slick clay.

Looking west from Badwater, the lowest point in the Western Hemisphere at 282 feet below sea level, the eye is drawn to what appears to be a shallow stream flowing across the valley floor. But this flow is a trompe l'oeil, a mirage caused by the strange terrain and deceptive colorings. Light plays upon the valley floor, and the mind spins as though caught in a color wheel, from the gray and gold of sunrise, to the lavender and purple of sunset, to the star-flecked ebony of night.

From the crest of the Black Mountains at Dante's View unfolds a panorama never to be forgotten. A vertical mile down lies the lowest spot on the continent. Opposite the overlook, across the valley, rise Telescope Peak and the snow-clad summits of the Panamints. Farther still, on the western horizon, loom the granite ramparts of the Sierra Nevada. North and south from Dante's View rises the Funeral Range. And from here, too, is the glimmer of that alkaline pool called Badwater—or is that just a mirage?

Americans looking for gold in California's mountains in 1849 were forced to cross the burning sands to avoid severe snowstorms in the nearby Sierra Nevada. Some perished along the way, and the land became known as Death Valley.

Many of Death Valley's topographical features are associated with hellish images—Funeral Mountains, Furnace Creek, Dante's View, Coffin Peak, and Devil's Golf Course—but the national park can be a place of serenity.

A multitude of living things have miraculously adapted to living in this land of little water, extreme heat, and high winds. Two dozen Death Valley plant species grow nowhere else on earth, including Death Valley sandpaper plant, Panamint locoweed, and napkin-ring buckwheat.

In spring, even this most forbidding of deserts breaks into bloom. The deep-blue pea-shaped flowers of the indigo bush brighten Daylight Pass. Lupine, paintbrush, and Panamint daisies grow on the lower slopes of the Panamint Range while Mojave wildrose and mariposa lily dot the higher slopes.

Two hundred species of birds are found in Death Valley. The brown whiplike stems of the creosote bush help shelter the movements of the kangaroo rat, desert tortoise, and antelope ground squirrel. Night covers the movements of the bobcat, fox, and coyote. Small bands of bighorn sheep roam remote slopes and peaks. Three species of desert pupfish, survivors from the Ice Age, are found in the valley's saline creeks and pools.

Death Valley celebrates life. Despite the outward harshness of this land, when you get to know the valley, you see it in a different light. As naturalist Joseph Wood Krutch put it: "Hardship looks attractive, scarcity becomes desirable, starkness takes on an unexpected beauty."

Eureka Dunes

Eureka Dunes Trail

Terrain: Massive white sand dunes, ½-mile wide, 3½ miles long.

Highlights: Tallest California sand dunes; a photographer's dream. Kids love it here.

Distance: 1 to 5 miles round-trip.

Degree of difficulty: Easy to moderate.

Between the Owens Valley and Death Valley, isolated and often overlooked Eureka Valley holds many surprises, chief among them the Eureka Dunes. The dunes, formerly known as the Eureka Dunes National Natural Landmark and administered by the Bureau of Land Management, were added to the expanded Death Valley National Park in 1994.

The dunes occupy the site of an ancient lake bed, whose shoreline can be identified to the northeast of the dunes. The onetime flat lake bed northwest of the dunes sometimes captures a little surface water; this happenstance delights photographers who focus their cameras on the water and capture a reflection of the Inyo Mountains.

The neighboring Last Chance Mountains gets their fair share of the meager rainfall in these parts—meaning the dunes are (relatively) well watered. Rainwater percolates downward, where it later nurtures some 50 dune plants even in the driest of years. Three species of flora occur nowhere else: Eureka Dunes milk vetch, Eureka dune grass, and the showy Eureka Dunes evening primrose, with its large white flowers.

Like their cousins the Kelso Dunes in Mojave National Preserve, the Eureka Dunes "boom." Low vibrational sounds are created when the wind-polished, well-rounded grains of sand slip-slide underfoot. The booming, which has been compared with the sound of a low-altitude airplane and a Tibetan gong, is louder in the Kelso Dunes.

It's not the noise of Eureka Dunes but their silence that impresses the hiker, however. The dunes, California's highest at nearly 700 feet high, are also impressive for their size.

The trailless walking is strictly free-form, both up and across the dunes. If you reach the top of the island of sand, you'll get a unique vista of Eureka Valley and the many mountains that surround it: the Last Chance Range to the northeast, the Saline Range to the west, the Inyo Mountains to the southwest.

Directions to trailhead: From the entrance station (fee) opposite Grapevine Campground, continue north on Highway 190 a short distance to a fork. The right fork leads to Scotty's Castle, but you continue toward Ubehebe Crater 2⅘ miles, then turn right onto dirt Death Valley Road. Drive 21 miles northwest to Crankshaft Junction. Bear left, continuing on Death Valley Road, which heads southwest up and over the Last Chance Range. (A few miles of the road through Hanging Rock Canyon are paved; the rest is dirt.) After 12³⁄₁₀ miles, turn left (south) onto South Eureka Road and travel 10⁷⁄₁₀ miles to the north end of the dunes and a road fork.

An ungraded road goes east to the north side (near interpretive signs) and primitive campsites. You can safely drive straight ahead to the northwest corner of the dunes. Avoid getting stuck by staying on the established roads.

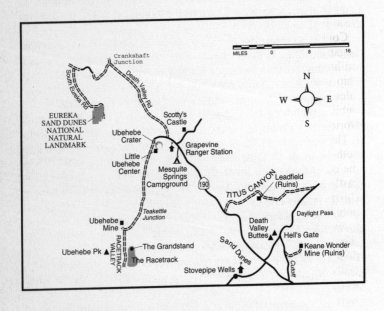

▲
Scotty's Castle
Windy Point Trail

Terrain: Developed/undeveloped Grapevine Canyon.
Highlights: Tour fantastic Moorish castle, surrounding environs.
Distance: From the castle to Scotty's grave is ¾-mile roundtrip.
Degree of difficulty: Easy.

Scotty's Castle, the Mediterranean-to-the-max mega-hacienda in the northern part of the park, is unabashedly Death Valley's premier tourist attraction. Visitors are wowed by the elaborate Spanish tiles, well-crafted furnishings, and innovative construction that included solar water-heating. Even more compelling is the colorful history of this villa in remote Grapevine Canyon.

Construction of the "castle"—officially, Death Valley Ranch—began in 1924. It was to be a winter retreat for eccentric Chicago millionaire Albert Johnson. The insurance tycoon's unlikely friendship with Walter Scott, a prospector, cowboy, and spinner of tall tales, put the $2.3 million structure on the map and captured the public's imagination. Scotty greeted visitors and told them fanciful stories from the early hard-rock-mining days of Death Valley.

The one-hour walking tour (fee) of Scotty's Castle is excellent, both for its inside look at the mansion and for what it reveals about the eccentricities of Johnson and Scotty. To learn more about the castle grounds, pick up the pamphlet *A Walking Tour of Scotty's Castle,* which leads you on an exploration from stable to swimming pool, from bunkhouse to powerhouse.

Another walk is the short hike through Tie Canyon Wash, which supplied tons and tons of sand and gravel for the castle's construction. Mixed with cement, these raw materials went into the castle walls, and into the unique concrete fenceposts, each bearing the letters *J* and *S*—for Albert Johnson and Death Valley Scotty. Winters were cold in the canyon and much wood was needed for the castle's many fireplaces. Johnson bought 70 miles' worth of railroad ties from the abandoned Bullfrog-Goldfield railroad. The ties, thousands of which are still stacked in Tie Canyon, cost him about a penny apiece.

Windy Point Trail, which leads to a cross marking Death Valley Scotty's grave, is a self-guided walk keyed to an interpretive pamphlet that gives an overview of the desert flora. The path skirts the cookhouse, unfortunately destroyed by fire in 1991 when a park service computer short-circuited. You'll see an intriguing solar water heater—very high-tech for its time and a useful conservation lesson for today.

Windy Point is, indeed, often windy, but it was actually named for Death Valley Scotty's dog, who lies buried next to his master.

Directions to trailhead: Scotty's Castle is located some 53 miles north of the park visitor center.

Touring Scotty's Castle—inside and out—is quite an adventure.

Ubehebe Crater

Little Hebe Crater Trail

> **Terrain:** Cinder-covered rims of volcanic craters.
> **Highlights:** Magnificent examples of volcanism.
> **Distance:** From Ubehebe Crater to Little Hebe Crater is 1 mile round-trip with 200-foot elevation gain.
> **Degree of difficulty:** Easy.

Add volcanism to the list of cataclysms such as earthquakes and flash floods that caused high-speed changes to the Death Valley landscape.

Little Hebe and Ubehebe are sometimes called explosion craters. One look and you know why. Hot magma rising from the depths of the earth met the ground water; the resultant steam blasted out a crater and scattered cinders.

To the native Shoshone of Death Valley, the crater was known as *Temp-pin-tta Wo' sah*, "Basket in the Rock"—an apt description indeed. Half-mile-in-diameter Ubehebe is not the only "basket" around; to the south is Little Hebe Crater, and a cluster of smaller craters.

When measured by geological time, the craters are quite young— a few thousand years old. Most of the cinders covering the 6-mile area are from Ubehebe.

Although many visitors are drawn to the rim of Ubehebe, few descend to the bottom of the crater. If you do, watch your footing; the crater wall is a loose mixture of gravel and cinders.

The more interesting walk is the ½-mile rim-to-rim route from Ubehebe to Little Hebe Crater.

Directions to trailhead: From the Grapevine Ranger Station at the north end of the park, continue north (don't take the right fork to Scotty's Castle) 2⅘ miles to the signed turnoff for Ubehebe Crater. Follow the turnoff 2½ miles to the crater parking area.

The walk: From the edge of 500-foot-deep Ubehebe Crater, join the south-trending path over loose cinders. The trail tops a couple of rises, then splits. You can either go down to Little Hebe or head farther south along the ridge.

Walk the perimeter of Little Hebe Crater and enjoy the views of the valley and of the Last Chance Range to the west.

⛰ Ubehebe Peak

Ubehebe Peak Trail

> **Terrain:** Rocky crest of Last Chance Range.
> **Highlights:** Grand views of Sierra Nevada summits, the Racetrack.
> **Distance:** From Racetrack parking area to summit is 5 miles round-trip with 2,000-foot elevation gain.
> **Degree of difficulty:** Strenuous.

Many a marvelous vista is the hiker's reward for climbing the steep trail to Ubehebe Peak, a remote summit in the equally remote Last Chance Range. The White Mountains Saline Valley and High Sierra are among the sights to be seen from the peak.

Ubehebe means "Big Basket" in the Shoshone language; such a name seems more appropriate to Ubehebe Crater 24 miles northeast of the rocky peak.

For most travelers, the attraction in this part of the park is not rarely visited Ubehebe Peak but a 3-mile mudflat known as the Racetrack. Rocks are pushed along the sometimes muddy surface by high winds, leaving long, faint tracks. Most of the tracks you're likely to see on the playa are made by smaller rocks, but over the years there have been reports of rocks weighing several hundred pounds skidding for ¼-mile.

The Grandstand, a rock outcropping at the northern end of the Racetrack, is an easy ½-mile walk from the pullout off Racetrack Valley Road. This pullout is also the trailhead for the hike to Ubehebe Peak.

The old miners' trail that leads to the crest is in fairly good condition. To reach the very top of Ubehebe Peak requires some rock scrambling (Class 2–3); however, traveling only as far as the crest delivers equally good views.

Directions to trailhead: From the Grapevine Ranger Station at the north end of the park, continue north (don't take the right fork to Scotty's Castle) 2⅘ miles to the signed turnoff for Ubehebe Crater. After 2½ miles the paved road ends with a left turn into the Ubehebe Crater parking lot, but you continue south 20 miles on the washboard-surfaced, occasionally rough Racetrack Valley Road to Tea Kettle Junction, colorfully decorated with teakettles. Bear right, traveling another 5⁷⁄₁₀ miles to a turnout on the right (west) side of the road opposite the Grandstand and the Racetrack.

The walk: After a brief, moderate ascent through a creosote-dotted alluvial fan, the path steepens as it begins climbing over the desert-varnished shoulder of the peak. Many a switchback brings you to the crest of the range, 1½ miles from the trailhead.

From the 5,000-foot crest, savor the panorama: the Inyo Mountains, the Racetrack, the Cottonwood Mountains, the snowcapped peaks of the High Sierra.

If you want to bag the peak, follow the trail as it climbs steeply along the crest, switchbacks some more, and reaches a rocky shoulder, where it fades away. You continue along the crest, dipping briefly, then rock-scrambling to the small summit area.

Saline Peak

Saline Peak Cross-country Route

Terrain: Saline Range on east side of Saline Valley.
Highlights: Saline Valley and High Sierra vistas.
Distance: From Saline-Eureka Corridor Road to Saline Peak
  is 9 miles round-trip (cross-country route) with 3,700-foot
  elevation gain.
Degree of difficulty: Strenuous.

With its salt marsh and sand dunes, dry lakes and hot springs, Saline Valley was a splendid 1994 addition to Death Valley National Park. The best view of the valley is from the Saline Range's high point, 7,063-foot Saline Peak.

Like so many other desert peaks, Saline lacks a trail to the summit; however, the intrepid hiker can improvise a cross-country route to the top.

On the drive through Saline Valley you'll pass Lower Warm Springs and Palm Spring. Hot-spring devotees have diverted hot water into several concrete tubs. These hot pools (unofficially clothing optional) and the primitive areas nearby have long been popular.

Directions to trailhead: From Highway 395 in Olancha, drive 30 miles east to signed Saline Valley turnoff and head north 4 miles. After 4 miles, bear right at a road fork. Continue another 10 miles, then bear right at another fork toward Hunter Mountain. Go 5 more miles, then veer left down Grapevine Canyon into Saline Valley and continue north to Painted Rock Canyon—the turnoff for Warm Spring Campground. It's miles to Lower Warm Springs, Palm Spring, and Upper Warm Spring. Follow the Saline-Eureka Valley Corridor Road, a very rough track (suitable only for high-clearance, or better yet, four-wheel-drive vehicles) that runs northeast some miles to the starting point for the climb.

The walk: The hike to Saline Peak is strictly a do-it-yourself proposition. First you ascend gradually across the valley floor to the peak's east ridge. Then you follow the ridge to the summit for grand views of the Saline Valley and the Inyo Mountains to the west. Peeking over the shoulder of the Inyo range is the mighty, snow-covered Sierra Nevada.

Titus Canyon

Titus Canyon Trail

> **Terrain:** Dramatic, high-walled canyon.
> **Highlights:** One of most scenic canyons in Death Valley; a geologic wonder.
> **Distance:** Through narrow part of canyon is 4 to 5 miles round-trip; to Klare Spring is 12 miles round-trip.
> **Degree of difficulty:** Moderate.

In Titus Canyon, gray and white cliffs, red and green hills, and fractured and contorted rocks point to the tremendous geologic forces that shaped the land we call Death Valley National Park.

Titus Canyon offers the hiker—and the motorist (more about vehicles in a moment)—a chance to explore one of Death Valley's scenic gems. Hikers enter a twisting narrows, where a block of the earth's crust has dropped down along fault lines below the surrounding mountain walls.

The canyon is named for Morris Titus, who in 1906 left the Nevada boomtown of Rhyolite (now a historic ghost town), near the California border, with a prospecting party. When the prospectors were camped in the canyon, water supplies dwindled. Titus left in search of water and help, and was never seen again.

Winding through the canyon is 28-mile Titus Canyon Road, a narrow, one-way dirt road. If you're visiting the canyon by vehicle, the park suggests using four-wheel drive, though the area is open to two-wheel-drive vehicles with good ground clearance. Check on road conditions at the park visitor center in Furnace Creek. Geology buffs will want to pick up a copy of the *Titus Canyon Road Guide* at the visitor center.

Allow 2 to 3 hours for the drive, which takes you through a variety of environments. A historic highlight en route is a stop at the ghost town of Leadfield. The town boomed in 1925 owing to the slick efforts of a promoter who controlled a very low grade deposit of lead ore. Soon a town was built in the narrow canyon; its population rapidly swelled to 300. A year later, the town was empty.

Today only a shack or two and some crumbling foundations mark Leadfield, but the road that serviced the mines and miners remains behind, beckoning to those who prospect for scenery.

While in theory, vehicles and hikers should not be sharing narrow thoroughfares, in practice, in Titus Canyon, the arrangement works okay. Those motorists who brave Titus Canyon are a courteous lot—and hikers can hear them coming from a long way off, thus avoiding potential mishaps.

Directions to trailhead: To reach the start of one-way Titus Canyon Road, from Highway 190, a few miles from Stovepipe Wells, head northeast on Highway 374 toward Beatty, Nevada, 25 miles away. About 4 miles short of Beatty is the signed turnoff for Titus Canyon.

You don't have to drive the 28-mile road to hike Titus Canyon. The lower part of Titus Canyon Road is two-way and takes you to the trailhead. From the junction of Highways 374 and 190, you'll head north 14 miles on 190 to Titus Canyon Road.

The walk: From the trailhead, it's moderate uphill walking along the gravel floor of the canyon. As you hike along you'll marvel at the awesome folding and faulting of the canyon's rock walls. For a moderate walk through the rock show, continue a couple of miles up-canyon and turn around.

More gung-ho hikers will keep trekking up Titus Canyon, which widens a bit. Nearly 6 miles out is Klare Spring, a water hole occasionally visited by a band of bighorn sheep.

Just beyond the spring is a wildly contorted section of canyon wall and a park service sign entitled "When Rocks Bend." Try to determine just which end of the rock formation is up, then head back down Titus Canyon to the trailhead.

Death Valley Buttes
Death Valley Buttes Trail

> **Terrain:** Isolated hills at the base of the Grapevine Mountains.
> **Highlights:** Dramatic views of the heart of Death Valley.
> **Distance:** From Hell's Gate to the top of the buttes is 4 miles round-trip with 900-foot elevation gain.
> **Degree of difficulty:** Moderate to strenuous cross-country travel.

Grand views of the central part of the national park are the hiker's reward for a trailless scramble to the top of Death Valley Buttes, three distinct hills at the base of the Grapevine Mountains. The sweeping panorama includes the valley floor and the Funeral and Panamint ranges.

Death Valley Buttes are actually part and parcel of the Grapevine Mountains. Continuing erosion of the range has left much rock debris at the base of the mountains; this alluvium is gradually burying the lower ridges, leaving behind isolated high points, of which the most prominent are the Death Valley Buttes.

The route to the buttes begins at Hell's Gate—named, the story goes, in 1905 by a teamster who was struck by the contrast between the relative cool of Boundary Canyon and the hotter area near the buttes. The mules would act startled and shake their heads at the sudden searing heat. "They thought they had stuck their noses through the gates of hell," the teamster is reported to have exclaimed.

Hell's Gate may seem an unlikely place in which to build a resort, but that's just what Bob Eichbaum dreamed of doing in the 1920s. In 1905 the young electrical engineer became enchanted with Death Valley when he helped construct an electrical plant in Rhyolite. After 20 years in the tourist business—operating a goat cart concession on Venice Beach and sightseeing tours on Catalina Island—he returned to Death Valley intent on building a grand hotel, "one of the wonders of the country." He planned to collect customers in Los Angeles and bus them to Hell's Gate, but bad roads doomed his plan and his resort was never built. (Eichbaum, however, did open the original Stovepipe Wells Hotel in 1926, as well as the Eichbaum Toll Road over Towne Pass into the valley.)

The cross-country route to the buttes is easy enough to accomplish. More difficult is the narrow, rocky ridge that must be traversed; it is best left to experienced hikers.

Directions to trailhead: From the Furnace Creek Visitor Center, drive north on Highway 190 for 11 miles. Veer right toward Beatty on the Daylight Pass Cutoff and travel northwest 10 miles to Hell's Gate, where you'll find a large parking area and picnic tables.

The walk: Walk southwest toward the buttes across rocky terrain dotted with creosote and beavertail cactus. Look for the remains of the phone line that crossed this land, connecting Rhyolite to civilization, such as it was, in the southwest.

After ½-mile, you leave behind this relatively gentle alluvial fan and strike south toward the ridge of the easternmost butte. Follow the rock crest westward, aided by an intermittent trail, to the 2,725-foot summit. Admire the barren Grapevine Mountains nearby and the equally austere Funeral Mountains extending southeast.

You can return the way you came, or continue to the next and highest butte. If you press on (only for experienced hikers), you'll descend the steep ridgeline west to a saddle, then ascend the narrow ridge ½-mile to Peak 3,017. Enjoy the view across the shimmering valley floor to the Panamint Mountains.

Keane Wonder Mine

Keane Wonder Mine Trail

Terrain: Steep creosote-flecked west slope of Funeral
  Mountains.
Highlights: Historic "sky railroad," great views.
Distance: 2 miles round-trip with 1,800-foot elevation gain.
Degree of difficulty: Short but strenuous.
Precautions: Stay away from dangerous shafts and tunnels.

One of the most noted mines in the Funeral Mountains was Homer
Wilson's Keane Wonder, which operated from 1903 to 1916. During its best years, the mine produced a quarter of a million dollars a
year in gold.

Even more noteworthy than the mine was "Death Valley's Sky
Railroad," a gravity-powered aerial tram that ran for a mile up the
precipitous slopes of the Funerals. The half-ton weight of the loaded
ore buckets descending to the mill raised the empties back up to the
mine.

The tram must have been an energy-saver for the miners who, if
they had been required to hike to work every day, would not have
been very productive. The 20-minute ride was exhilarating to say
the least for mine visitors, who sat on a little iron bench, legs dangling hundreds of feet above jagged rocks. Few visitors requested a
second ride.

While the mine was profitable, most of the money went to pay off
loans, purchase machinery, and search (unsuccessfully) for more
pockets of gold. A failed bank, questionable stock transactions, and
insider trading—legal battles for control of the Keane Wonder
Mine—outlasted the mine itself.

Hikers can view some old mill ruins and follow a trail along the
route of the old tramway, past a series of wooden towers, to the
mine. It's a stiff climb; you might wish the tram was still running.

Directions to trailhead: From Furnace Creek, follow Highway
190 north 10 miles, veer right onto the Daylight Pass Cutoff, and
drive 5⁷⁄₁₀ miles to the signed turnoff to Keane Wonder Mine. Turn
east and drive 2⅖ miles to road's end at the mine.

The walk: Follow an old roadbed, then join the footpath and begin an extremely steep ascent. After ½-mile the grade lessens, and another ½-mile of more moderate hiking takes you to the top of the aerial tramway. From the ruins of the upper tram station, partake of the grand valley views.

Only ruins remains of colorful mining days gone by.

Death Valley Dunes
Dunes Trail

> **Terrain:** Sand dunes, 14 square miles of them.
> **Highlights:** Fun, frolic in the sand.
> **Distance:** 2 to 4 miles round-trip.
> **Degree of difficulty:** Easy.
> **Precautions:** Wear shoes; sand surface is very hot.

A 14-square-mile field of dunes and some bizarre geology are some of the attractions of walking around the Stovepipe Wells area of Death Valley National Park.

Hiking the dunes is most fun in the cooler morning and late afternoon hours. At these times, the dunes are at their most photogenic, too: the light is softer, the shadows longer.

Death Valley's dunes are formed in much the same way as those megadunes in the Middle East and North Africa.

What nature needs to form dunes in fairly simple: a source of sand, wind to separate the sand from gravel, more wind to roll the sand along into drifts, and still more wind, perhaps in the form of a back draft, to keep the dunes in place.

Death Valley's dunes lie between Towne Pass on the west and Daylight Pass to the east; there's quite a sand-laden draft between the two passes.

"Dune Speak" is a colorful language, a vocabulary of windward and leeward faces, black patches and Chinese walls, blow sand and sand shadows.

The slip face of the dunes (away from the wind) is very steep, but never steeper than thirty-four degrees—known as the angle of repose. Angles steeper than this trigger an avalanche, which reduces the angle a degree or three.

As you hike the dunes, you'll notice blow sand (loose, very fine particles) piled on the leeward side of plants; these piles are known as sand shadows.

Death Valley's dunes are subbarchan, or crescent-shaped. The sand dunes are actually tiny pieces of rock, most of them quartz fragments.

Near the dunes are some weird natural features. Those surrealistic-looking cornstalks you see across Highway 190 from the dunes are actually clumps of arrowweed. The Devil's Cornfields are perched on wind- and water-eroded pedestals.

Fringing the dunes are expanses of dry mud that have cracked and buckled into interesting patterns. These mud sink areas and the edges of the dunes themselves are good places to look for the tracks of the few desert creatures able to survive in the harsh environment—most notably rabbits and kangaroo rats.

Your hike into the dunes is exactly what you make of it—short or long, a direct or indirect route to the higher sand formations. Figure on 4 miles at the most to climb up, down, and around the taller dunes and return. Remember that exploring the dunes often involves a two-steps-forward, one-step-backward kind of hiking, so pace yourself accordingly.

Directions to trailhead: Take Highway 190 6 miles east of Stovepipe Wells village to the signed turnoff for the dunes. Turn north on the good dirt road and follow it a short distance to the dune picnic area.

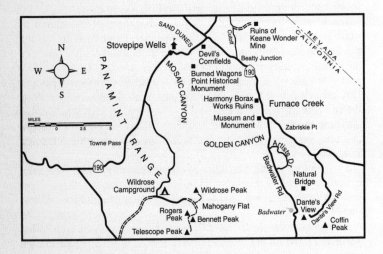

Burned Wagons Point

Burned Wagons Point Trail

Terrain: Valley floor near Stovepipe Wells.
Highlights: Historic route, camp of Death Valley forty-niners.
Distance: From Highway 190 to Burned Wagons Point is 4½ miles round-trip.
Degree of difficulty: Moderate.

Fearful of the terrible cold and snows of the High Sierra, and mindful of the fate of the Donner Party three years earlier, a group of California-bound pioneers took a more southerly route, ending up hot, hungry, and lost in the autumn of 1849. A splinter group of these pioneers, known as the Jayhawkers, camped in the area of present-day Stovepipe Wells. Here they slaughtered the last of their oxen and burned their wagons to smoke and preserve the meat.

Today, at Burned Wagons Point, you can imagine the fear these emigrants felt as they looked across the bleak valley floor toward the seemingly insurmountable Panamint Mountains. As you hike to the pioneers' camp, you can also get a taste of their lonely journey—which in this case ended happily with the pioneers finding a way out of the valley through Towne Pass.

Directions to trailhead: From Highway 190 in Stovepipe Wells, park opposite the entrance to the Sand Dunes Picnic Area. Across the highway from the entrance is an old dirt road, the trail to Burned Wagons Point.

The walk: The trail starts south across the valley floor. A ½-mile along you'll pass mesquite-covered mounds of sand.

About 1½ miles from the trailhead the road enters a cluster of low hills. The main route continues southeast, but you'll join a narrow westbound wash that penetrates a long ridge on your right. This wash soon routes you through the hills. You'll then joint a faint path angling south ¾-mile to Burned Wagons Point.

Immediately west of Burned Wagons Point, marked with a sign, is McClean Spring, a modest pool of brackish water believed to have been used as a water supply by the forty-niners.

Also nearby is pickleweed- and salt grass–lined Salt Creek. (See Salt Creek walk.)

Mosaic Canyon

Mosaic Canyon Trail

> **Terrain:** Narrow, twisting canyon.
> **Highlights:** Mosaics of colorful rock fragments decorate canyon walls.
> **Distance:** 4 miles round-trip through the "narrows."
> **Degree of difficulty:** Easy to moderate.

Some Death Valley canyons deliver the scenery promised in their names—Golden, Red Wall, and Corkscrew, to name a few.

Mosaic Canyon is another fine example of truth-in-labeling. The canyon, located near Stovepipe Wells, displays mosaics of water-polished white, gray, and black rock.

Nature has cemented the canyon's stream gravel into mosaics large and small. It's easy to imagine you've entered an art gallery when you view the mosaics on the canyon walls; not only are nature's works of art on display, but the long, narrow, white marble walls of the canyon seem quite "gallery"-like.

Mosaic is one of those desert canyons with an hourglass shape: a fairly wide head and mouth connected by a narrow, deep gorge. This means that during a storm, rainwater collects on the broad surface at the head of the canyon, then funnels through the narrow midsection at high velocity. The water, laden with rock debris, sculpts the canyon into its photogenic form and polishes the rock walls.

(By the way, a narrow canyon like Mosaic is the very last place you want to be in a rainstorm!)

Mosaic Canyon is an ideal family outing. Rangers lead interpretive walks through the canyon. Check at the main park visitor center in Furnace Creek or the small center at Stovepipe Wells for schedules of guided walks.

Serious hikers can persevere several more miles up ever-steeper slopes toward the head of Mosaic Canyon or enjoy the rock-climbing challenge afforded by rugged tributary canyons.

Directions to trailhead: From the west end of Stovepipe Wells village, turn south on the signed dirt road for Mosaic Canyon. Follow the bumpy road (suitable for passenger cars with good ground clearance) 2½ miles to its end at a parking lot.

The walk: Walk up the sand-and-gravel canyon bottom. In a short time, you'll round a bend and enter a corridor of polished rock. At the next bend you'll climb a dry waterfall. The farther you go, the higher the walls get, exposing more and more of the mosaics that gave the canyon its name.

After ¾-mile, the canyon opens up into a wider wash. As you hike along, marveling at the mosaics, you'll notice that a couple of minor canyons join Mosaic on your right. These can be explored if you have the inclination and determination.

As the wash narrows again about 2 miles from the trailhead, some hikers may get the feeling that they're beginning to do more rock climbing than hiking. This is a good turnaround point; stop while you're having a good time and before you exceed your abilities.

Salt Creek

Salt Creek Interpretive Trail

Terrain: Pickleweed-lined banks of Salt Creek.
Highlights: Boardwalk nature trail, viewing rare desert
  pupfish.
Distance: 1 to 2 miles round-trip.
Degree of difficulty: Easy.

Salt Creek is the home of the Salt Creek pupfish, found nowhere
else on earth. A nature trail along a boardwalk tells the amazing
story of *Cyprinodon salinus.*

Many desert creatures display unusual adaptations to the rigors of
life in arid lands and changes in their environment, but few have
had to make more remarkable adjustments than the little Salt Creek
pupfish.

Thousands of years ago a large freshwater lake covered the area.
Gradually this lake became smaller and smaller while the lake's
salinity greatly increased. Many plants and animals failed to adapt
to an environment radically different from the one in which their
forebears existed.

But the pupfish adapted—it evolved the ability to filter saltwater,
remove the excess salt, and excrete it through kidneys or gills. And
the inch-long fish, used to a lot of water and a fairly constant temperature, adapted to life in a relatively tiny amount of water that
varies in temperature from near freezing to nearly 100°F.

Once the pupfish were so numerous that the valley's native peoples
harvested them for food. They were still numerous when the 1938
WPA Guide to Death Valley described them: "Prospectors amuse
themselves by holding a pan full of crumbs just below the surface
and watching the greedy fish crowd in to eat. They come so rapidly
and in such numbers, that they sometimes make small waves."

Alas, by the 1970s, the pupfish was on the endangered species
list. The pupfish population has since rebounded thanks to habitat-
improvement efforts by wildlife biologists and a park service–built
boardwalk that reduces the impact of visitors on the soft creek banks.

The best time to see the fish is from mid-April to September. In
spring a million pupfish might be wriggling in the creek; by summer's end, a few thousand remain.

Directions to trailhead: From Highway 190, 13 miles north of Furnace Creek, turn west onto a dirt road leading to the Salt Creek parking area.

The walk: Pick up a copy of the park service's *Salt Creek Nature Trail* pamphlet and begin your stroll along the boardwalk. At the northern end of the loop, leave the boardwalk and take the footpath continuing north along the east side of the creek. Walk another ½-mile or so along the nearly 30-mile-long creek. You'll see more pupfish, as well as birds ranging from snipes to great blue herons.

Harmony Borax Works

Harmony Borax Works Trail

Terrain: Salt flats, the odd "haystacks."
Highlights: Colorful walk into Death Valley history.
Distance: 2⅗ miles round-trip; to haystacks is 5 miles round-trip.
Degree of difficulty: Easy walk through Borax; moderate walk to haystacks.

Death Valley National Park—it seems almost a contradiction in terms, particularly when you hike out to the old Harmony Borax Works—a rock-salt landscape as tortured as you'll ever find.

A park? Surely if the notion of a park was ever mentioned to one of the rough drivers of the 20-mule-team borax wagons that crossed Death Valley, his response would be unprintable in a family guidebook.

But back to borax. In Death Valley, strangely enough, the borax story and the park story are almost inseparable. Borax supersalesman Stephen T. Mather became the first director of the National Park Service in 1916.

"White gold," Death Valley prospectors called it. Borax is not exactly a glamorous substance, but it has proved to be a profitable one. From 1883 to 1888, more than 20 million pounds of borax were transported from the Harmony Borax Works.

Transport of the borax was the stuff of legends, too. The famous 20-mule teams hauled the huge loaded wagons 165 miles to the rail station at Mojave.

Down-on-his-luck prospector Aaron Winters first discovered borax on the salt flats in Furnace Creek in 1881. He was ecstatic when a San Francisco investor, William Coleman, purchased his rights to the borax field for $20,000. Coleman capitalized construction of the Harmony Borax Works, an endeavor that depended first and foremost on the labors of Chinese-Americans who gathered the fibrous clusters of borate, called "cottonballs."

After purification at the borax works, the substance was loaded into custom 15-foot-long wagons to be hauled by 10 pairs of mules. The animals were controlled by a long jerk line and legendary muleskinner profanity.

To learn more about this colorful era, visit the Borax Museum at Furnace Creek Ranch and the park visitor center, also located in Furnace Creek.

Directions to trailhead: To reach Harmony Borax Works from Furnace Creek, follow Highway 190 for 1½ miles to the signed turn-off on the west side of the highway.

The walk: A short trail with interpretive signs leads past the ruins of the old borax refinery and some outlying buildings.

The main trail leads 1³⁄₁₀ miles over the salt flats. You'll travel through a wash to trail's end at a wooden post. From here it's less than 200 yards to the edge of the salt marsh where borax was mined.

Adventurous hikers can make the trailless trek across sometimes spongy terrain to the borax haystacks, 2-foot-high piles of sodium/calcium borate balls stacked here in the 1880s by Chinese laborers to prove claim assessment work. The hike—and the photo opportunities—are particularly good early in the morning.

Interpretive exhibits, including these borax wagons, give a glimpse into a once-profitable industry, as well as the lives of the people who toiled there.

Golden Canyon, Zabriskie Point

Golden Canyon Trail

> **Terrain:** Alluvial fan, dramatic cliffs.
> **Highlights:** Grand view, display of color from purple to gold as sun passes over Golden Canyon.
> **Distance:** To Red Cathedral is 2½ miles round-trip; to Zabriskie Point is 6 miles round-trip with 700-foot elevation gain.
> **Degree of difficulty:** Moderate.

Before sunrise, photographers set up their tripods at Zabriskie Point and aim their cameras down at the pale mudstone hills of Golden Canyon and the great valley beyond. The panoramic view of Golden Canyon through a lens is magnificent, but don't miss getting right into the canyon itself—which is only possible by hitting the trail.

Until the rainy winter of 1976, Golden Canyon had a road running through it. A desert deluge washed away the road, and it's been a trail ever since.

The first mile of Golden Canyon Trail is a self-guided interpretive trail. Pick up a copy of the National Park Service's *Trail Guide to Golden Canyon* pamphlet, available at visitor centers. Stops in the guide are keyed to numbers along the trail, and will likely tell you more about Miocene volcanic activity, Jurassic granitic intrusion, and Precambrian erosion than you ever wanted to know.

At the end of the nature trail, the path branches. One fork heads for Red Cathedral, also called Red Cliffs. The red color is essentially iron oxide—rust—produced by weathering of rocks with a high iron content.

A second trail branch climbs 2 miles through badlands to Zabriskie Point. While it's true that you can drive to Zabriskie Point, you'll appreciate the view much more by sweating up those switchbacks on foot.

Directions to trailhead: From the Furnace Creek Visitor Center, drive south on Highway 190, forking right onto Highway 178. The signed Golden Canyon Trail is on your left, 3 miles from the visitor center.

The walk: From the parking lot, hike up the alluvial fan into the canyon. Marvel at the tilted, faulted rock walls as they close in around you. Notice the ripple marks, created long ago by water lapping at the shore of an ancient lake.

Deeper and deeper into the badlands you ascend. Watch for white crystalline outcroppings of borax—the stuff of 20-mule-team fame.

At the end of the nature trail, you can continue up the main canyon ¼-mile to the old Golden Canyon parking lot. The trail narrows and you continue by squeezing through boulders and ascending a short ladder to the base of Red Cathedral, a colorful natural amphitheater.

Returning to the trail fork, this time you'll follow the trail signed with the international hiker's symbol and begin climbing toward Manly Beacon, a pinnacle of gold clay. The trail crests at the shoulder of the beacon, then descends into the badlands.

Watch for park service signs to stay on the trail, which is a bit difficult to follow as it marches up and down the severely eroded siltstone hills.

A final steep grade brings you to Zabriskie Point, named for Christian Brevoort Zabriskie, one of the early heads of Death Valley borax operations. Enjoy the grand view of the valley, framed by the badlands just below and the Panamint Mountains to the west. Walk back the way you came.

A sunrise walk through Golden Canyon shows Death Valley in a special light.

37

Desolation Canyon

Desolation Canyon Trail

Terrain: Broad alluvial fan, narrow canyon.
Highlights: Fascinating geology.
Distance: 4 miles round-trip.
Degree of difficulty: Moderate.

Deeply eroded hills, a rainbow of color on the lower slopes of the Black Mountains, and a twisted canyon so narrow you can reach out and touch its walls are among the highlights of a walk to and through Desolation Canyon.

The canyon is isolated and austere in places, but no more desolate than any other in the rugged foothills south of Furnace Creek. Desolation, like better-known Black Mountains canyons, offers a marvelous geology lesson to the willing walker.

This hike begins by following a broad alluvial fan, then penetrates narrow Desolation Canyon.

Directions to trailhead: From the junction of Highway 190 and Badwater Road near the Furnace Creek Inn, take the latter road 3 miles and park across from the DESOLATION CANYON sign. This walk follows the dirt road heading east.

The walk: Follow the old dirt road up the rocky, fan-shaped alluvium sprinkled with desert holly. After ½-mile, the road forks. Take the left fork and begin a mellow, ½-mile ascent, curving south to road's end at the base of some eroded hills. Angle 50 yards east to the mouth of Desolation Canyon wash.

Go right and follow the wash into the hills. After ¼-mile the walls of the canyon close in. The soft walls, dramatically sculpted by rushing water, soar more than a hundred feet above you.

Keep right at each of the forks in the twisted canyon to stay with the main wash. A ½-mile into Desolation Canyon are a couple of minor (3 to 5 feet high) dry cascades. This walk ends in a small box canyon about a mile from where you left the dirt road.

Natural Bridge

Natural Bridge Trail

> **Terrain:** Wash, grotto.
> **Highlights:** Natural bridge.
> **Distance:** ½-mile round-trip.
> **Degree of difficulty:** Easy.

The short path off Badwater Road offers the walker a little bit of southern Utah—an eroded canyon rim and a large natural bridge formation.

Long ago, water surged through a canyon wall, stripping away weaker strata and leaving behind a 50-foot-high rock bridge spanning the canyon.

Beyond the bridge, you can explore other water-cut formations—grottoes and benches, chutes and spillways.

Directions to trailhead: From Badwater Road, 15 miles south of the Furnace Creek Visitor Center, follow the signed dirt road 3 miles to the Natural Bridge trailhead.

Coffin Peak

Coffin Peak Trail

Terrain: Mile-high Black Mountains on southeast boundary of national park.

Highlights: Same panorama as Dante's View without the crowds.

Distance: From picnic area below Dante's View to Coffin Peak is 2½ miles with 300-foot elevation gain.

Degree of difficulty: Moderate.

Make no mistake: Dante's View offers one of Death Valley's finest panoramas. The trouble is, you can drive to the viewpoint—and thousands of motorists do, meaning your chances for quiet contemplation of the desert below are about as slim as the possibility of rainfall.

For the hiker, there is an alternative: Coffin Peak, offering the same great view as Dante's without the crowds.

The 5,503-foot peak (a smidgen higher than 5,475-foot Dante's View) is situated in the relatively little traveled Black Mountains that extend along the southeastern boundary of the national park.

In addition to Dante's View, the other major visitor attraction in the Black Mountains is Greenwater, where a few ruins and building foundations are all that remain of a copper-mining boomtown. The hype after the 1905 discovery of copper attracted a thousand people and soon Greenwater had stores, saloons, a post office, and even two newspapers and a men's magazine. What Greenwater lacked, however, was quality ore, and by 1908 it had become a ghost town.

Hikers experienced with cross-country travel will be most comfortable with the trailless trek to Coffin Peak; however, the less experienced can set out with the assurance that this walk for the most part stays within sight of Dante's View Road.

Directions to trailhead: From the Badwater Road–Highway 190 junction just south of the Furnace Creek Visitor Center, drive 10⅓ miles on Highway 190 toward Death Valley Junction. Turn right on Dante's View Road and continue 12⅗ miles (⅗-mile short of Dante's View). Turn left and park in the wide turnout, which has pit toilets and a picnic table.

The walk: From the picnic site, you'll parallel Dante's View Road, ascending a minor hill dotted with Mormon tea. Dodging spiny shrubs, follow the ridge crest as it bends southeast and climbs to the top of a 5,360-foot hill.

You'll continue east among handsome desert varnish–stained boulders, savoring the valley views. Topping another hill, you descend a short distance northeastward to a saddle, then climb again to Peak 5484.

Now you follow the crest south, then east, toward the conical summit of Coffin Peak. Your view encompasses the Black Mountains, south and north, the Funeral Mountains to the northeast, and the Greenwater Valley, green indeed with creosote, to the southeast. The shimmering valley floor, backed by the high Panamint Mountains to the west, completes the panoramic view.

Well, not quite. Just to the northwest is Dante's View, swarming with sightseers. After enjoying the view, return the way you came.

Darwin Falls

Darwin Falls Trail

Terrain: Year-round creek and waterfall.
Highlights: Surprising oasis, good bird-watching.
Distance: 1½ miles round-trip.
Degree of difficulty: Easy.

Tucked away in what appears to be a forlorn mountain range on the east side of the Panamint Valley is a year-round creek and waterfall. Darwin Falls and the mini-oasis surrounding it are small reminders of the surprises found off the main Mojave roads.

The falls are fed by an underground spring bubbling to the surface of the volcanic rock floor of Darwin Canyon. Wildlife and more than 80 species of birds find water and shelter at the cottonwood- and willow-fringed oasis.

During the 19th-century boomtown days of Darwin, a Chinese-American farmer grew vegetables in a rich patch of earth below the falls and sold his produce to the miners. For more than 100 years, visitors have enjoyed bathing in the stone basins in the canyon bottom.

Every Eden has its serpent, and in the case of Darwin Falls evil incarnate is the salt cedar tamarisk, an aggressive weed that prevents animals from reaching the water. Not only is the tamarisk fast-growing, it's a huge water consumer. Worse yet, the plant drops salty leaves that kill surrounding native vegetation. Thanks to the efforts of the Bureau of Land Management, the Sierra Club, and other conservation groups, much tamarisk has been removed from the Darwin Falls area.

The best time for a visit is spring when the creek flow is the greatest, the falls at their fullest. Forget hiking in the summer. At 3,100 feet in elevation, Darwin Falls is far from the hottest place in the Mojave, but because of the presence of the water, it's horribly humid.

Directions to trailhead: From Highway 395 in Olancha, head east on Highway 190 for 44 miles to tiny Panamint Springs. Turn right on Darwin Canyon Road and drive 2½ miles. At a fork, bear right and continue ³⁄₁₀-mile to the parking area.

The walk: It's dry going when you first walk the canyon bottom. Soon, though, you'll notice some wet sand, then spot a trickle of water. A ¼-mile along, the canyon narrows and you'll begin walking alongside a little creek. Ferns, reeds, and monkey flowers line the creek. The path ends at a 30-foot waterfall.

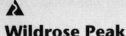

Wildrose Peak

Wildrose Peak Trail

Terrain: Pinyon pine and juniper woodland on crest of Panamints.
Highlights: Awesome panoramas.
Distance: 8⅖ miles round-trip with 2,300-foot elevation gain.
Degree of difficulty: Fairly strenuous.
Precautions: Snow covers summit and trail November through May.

Death Valley and Panamint Valley views are awesome from the summit of Wildrose Peak. The 9,064-foot peak in the middle of the Panamint Mountains beckons the hiker with a well-maintained trail and glorious views coming and going.

The Panamints are known as the wettest mountain range in Death Valley—a small claim to fame, to be sure, in the midst of one of America's most arid lands; nevertheless, there's enough precipitation in the form of rain and snow to nurture stands of pinyon pine and juniper and to water the "wildrose," the spring-blooming cliffrose that brightens the mountain.

In summer, when temperatures climb to more than 110°F on the floor of Death Valley, Wildrose Peak remains a pleasant place to walk. The peak and upper parts of the trail are snowbound in winter; however, Wildrose is walkable a bit earlier in spring than neighboring Telescope Peak (11,049 feet), which typically remains mantled in snow well into May.

The trailhead alone is worth the trip. Here you'll find 10 charcoal kilns, built in the 1870s to make charcoal from the trees growing in Wildrose Canyon. Charcoal was carried by mules from the giant beehive-shaped stone kilns to the Modock Mine, located in the Argus Range 25 miles away.

Directions to trailhead: From Highway 178, 52 miles from Highway 395, turn right at the signed paved road for Wildrose and proceed 9½ miles northwest to a junction with Mahogany Flat Road. Turn right, soon passing Wildrose Campground, and travel 6 miles (the last 2 miles on a dirt road) to a wide turnout for the charcoal kilns and parking for Wildrose Peak–bound hikers.

If you're journeying from the "main" part of Death Valley, travel 9 miles from Stovepipe Wells south on Highway 190 to Wildrose Road. Turn left and drive south 21 miles to Mahogany Flat Road.

The walk: Join the signed trail northwest of the charcoal kilns and begin your ascent above Wildrose Canyon. As you pass in and out of a pinyon and juniper woodland, enjoy the great views of High Sierra peaks, including mighty Mount Whitney. The path descends briefly into a wooded canyon, then climbs northeast.

About 2 miles out, the path reaches a saddle at the crest of the Panamints. Following the crest, the trail serves up great vistas of Death Valley shimmering in the heat eight thousand feet below, as well as over-the-shoulder views of Telescope Peak.

Vigorous switchbacks lead past wind-bent pinyon pines to the small, flat summit. The fantastic view takes in most of 90-mile-long Death Valley with the Amargosa Range beyond and Furnace Creek appearing as a green island on the vast salt flats. To the west are the saw-tooth summits of the Sierra Nevada.

These charcoal kilns have dominated the landscape for more than a century.

Telescope Peak

Telescope Peak Trail

Terrain: Bristlecone pine–dotted top of the Panamint Mountains.

Highlights: National park high point, magnificent vistas, one of California's truly great hikes.

Distance: To Rogers and Bennett peaks is 7 miles round-trip with 1,800-foot elevation gain; to Telescope Peak is 14 miles round-trip with 3,000-foot gain.

Degree of difficulty: Strenuous.

Precautions: Peak often snow-covered from November to mid-May. Check with park for latest trail conditions.

Most park visitors are content to stop their cars at Badwater, 282 feet below sea level, and look up at Telescope Peak, the greatest vertical rise in the lower 48 states. For the serious hiker, however, the challenge of climbing 11,049-foot Telescope Peak and looking down at Death Valley will prove irresistible. The views from Telescope Peak Trail include Badwater, low point of the continental United States, and Mount Whitney, the continental high point.

The trail starts where most trails end—1½ miles in the sky—and climbs a sagebrush- and pinyon pine–dotted hogback ridge to the pinnacle that is Telescope Peak. The well-maintained trails up Telescope and Wildrose peaks offer a distinctly different hiking experience than other park trails—which, for the most part, are of two types: nature–interpretive trails or cross-country routes through canyons or washes.

Magnificent vistas from the below-sea-level salt pans to the snowy summits of the Sierra Nevada reward the hardy hiker who ascends Telescope Peak. The 360-degree panorama inspired one W. T. Henderson, the first to climb the great mountain in 1860, to declare: "You can see so far, it's just like looking through a telescope."

The best times to make the climb are from about mid-May to November. During the colder months, Telescope Peak and much of the trail is covered in snow. Try to begin your hike at dawn, both to savor the sunrise and to allow sufficient time for the long journey.

Directions to trailhead: From Highway 178, 50 miles northeast of Highway 395 and Ridgecrest, turn right on Wildrose Canyon

Road and follow it 9 miles to road's end at Mahogany Flat Campground. Park at the campground.

The walk: The path climbs over pinyon pine–forested slopes and soon offers dramatic views of Death Valley and the Furnace Creek area. After 2 miles, the trail gains the spine of a ridge and soon a second valley comes into view: Panamint.

Three miles of moderate climbing brings you to a saddle between Rogers Peak and Bennett Peak. You can strike cross-country to reach the antennae-crowned summit, which stands about 400 feet higher than the trail. To reach Bennett Peak, continue on the main trail to a second saddle, then ascend cross-country past stands of limber pine to the top.

Telescope Peak Trail's final third is steep and remarkable. The path zigzags up the peak's steep east side, ascending through a stunted forest of limber and bristlecone pine.

From atop the peak, the far-reaching views include the White Mountains to the north and the High Sierra to the northeast. Off in those two patches of purple haze are Las Vegas far to the east and the San Gabriel Mountains above Los Angeles to the southwest.

The gnarled bristlecone pine clings to life in the harshest of lands.

Bird's-eye view of the West Mojave Desert from Saddleback Butte.

2. West Mojave Desert

Topographically, the East and West Mojave are quite different. The West presents great sandscapes, with many flat areas and some isolated ridges and buttes. The East Mojave is more mountainous.

On the fringe of the Los Angeles metropolis is the deep, rock-walled gorge of Soledad Canyon where bandito Tiburcio Vasquez fled the law, finding refuge amid rocks known as Robber's Roost. Because Vasquez hid here before his capture in the Santa Monica Mountains (he was hanged in San Jose in 1875), the sandstone crags were named after him.

Situated south of the Tehachapi Mountains and northwest of the San Gabriel Mountains, the Antelope Valley makes up the western frontier of the Mojave Desert. The rapidly expanding cities of Palmdale, Lancaster, and Victorville are located here.

The Antelope Valley's natural attractions include a reserve for the state's official flower, the California poppy, and another reserve for the endangered desert tortoise. Other parks preserve a Joshua tree woodland (Saddleback Butte State Park) and display the remarkable earthquake-fractured geology of this desert (Devil's Punchbowl County Park).

Joshua trees thrive in the valley. Palmdale, established in 1886, was named for the Joshuas; settlers mistakenly figured the spiky trees were palms. Saddleback Butte was originally named Joshua Tree State Park when it was created in 1960. The name was changed to avoid confusion with Joshua Tree National Monument.

When the Los Angeles to San Francisco rail line was constructed through the valley in the 1870s, it completely changed the ecology of the West Mojave. Because the Antelope Valley, a natural reservoir, had extensive groundwater, farmers grew alfalfa. Hay was supplied to dairy farmers in Los Angeles until well into the 1920s.

The spartan-looking valley once supported thousands of pronghorn antelope—hence the name Antelope Valley—and the numerous Native American tribes who hunted them. The railroad tracks interrupted the antelopes' migration, thus dooming the animals. They could easily cross the tracks, but instinct prevented them from doing so; they soon perished from exposure to harsh winters and the shrinkage of their habitat.

The California poppy blooms on many a grassy slope in the Golden State, but only in the Antelope Valley does the showy flower blanket whole hillsides in such brilliant orange sheets. Surely the finest concentration of California's state flower (during a good wild-flower year) is preserved at the California State Poppy Reserve in the Mojave Desert west of Lancaster.

North of the Antelope Valley are more wonders of the West Mojave: the Ancient Bristlecone Pine Forest on the slopes of the White Mountains, the lava flows of Fossil Falls, the bizarre science-fiction landscape of Trona Pinnacles.

The endangered desert tortoise is protected in its own federally designated Natural Area.

Ancient Bristlecone Pine Forest
Methuselah Trail

> **Terrain:** Basin and range, rugged mountain crests.
> **Highlights:** World's oldest living trees.
> **Distance:** 4½ miles round-trip.
> **Degree of difficulty:** Moderate.
> **Precautions:** High-altitude (9,000 to 10,000 feet) hiking.

High on the stony, storm-battered crests of the White Mountains, east of Bishop, grow the oldest trees on earth. These 4,000-year-old trees are bristlecone pines, which survive—in fact, thrive—in conditions that doom most other life.

The bristlecones are protected by the 28,000-acre Ancient Bristlecone Pine Forest, set aside in 1958. The forest, which crowns the White Mountains, is under the jurisdiction of the Inyo National Forest.

Bristlecone pines are found in other parts of the Great Basin, in eastern California, Nevada, and Utah, but the pines in the White Mountains are by far the oldest.

Bristlecones are old, but they're not very tall—only 25 feet or so. And they're slow growers, sometimes expanding only one inch in diameter every hundred years. Some sapling-sized specimens are actually hundreds of years old.

The pines are wonderfully gnarled and contorted—a photographer's delight. Some assume a sumo wrestler's stance; others grow nearly parallel with the ground. Their trunks and limbs have been sanded and polished by windblown pebbles and ice.

The name bristlecone comes from the foxtaillike branches with short needles. The cones themselves are purple when young, turning to a chocolate color when mature.

Oddly enough, the trees thrive where climatic conditions are most severe, where they are most exposed to the fury of winter storms. Bristlecones clinging to the high peaks live longer than those growing in lower, more sheltered places. The most ancient *Pinus longaeva* manage to gather nutrients from the poorest limestone soil.

The oldest of the tribe is Methuselah, about 4,700 years old. Many trees in both Schulman and Patriarch groves are 4,000 years old and still growing.

For many years, bristlecones were thought to be not only the oldest living trees, but the oldest living things on earth. More recently, botanists have come to believe that the oldest flora award should go to some of the creosote bushes growing in the Soggy Dry Lake area of the Mojave Desert. Dubbed "King Clone," the creosote are estimated to be more than 10,000 years old.

Geologists categorize the White Mountains, where the bristlecones grow, as basin-and-range terrain. The mountains rise quickly and dramatically nearly 2 miles above the desert floor. Summit views of the surrounding desert are superb.

Two trails explore Schulman Grove, named in honor of Dr. Edward Schulman, the scientist who in the 1950s first figured the advanced age of the bristlecones. Bristlecone Discovery Trail is a 1-mile self-guided loop suitable for the whole family. Numbered posts correspond to descriptions in a pamphlet available at the trailhead. Along the trail is Pine Alpha, the first 4,000-year-old bristlecone discovered by Schulman.

Methuselah Trail is a 4½-mile loop through Bristlecone Forest. It features close-up views of the trees and far-reaching panoramas of mountains and desert. As 4½-mile hikes go, this one seems longer, because of both the shortness of breath caused by high altitude and the many photo opportunities en route.

Methuselah Trail winds through some of the most beautiful parts of Schulman Grove, then climbs to a ridge offering views of the Inyo and Last Chance mountains. An interpretive brochure for the Methuselah Trail is available at the trailhead.

Truly heroic hikers will relish the challenge of reaching the summit of White Mountain, the namesake peak of the range. From Schulman Grove, you drive 13 miles up the road to Patriarch Grove, then 4 more miles to the trailhead. A 7½-mile trail leads to the top of 14,246-foot White Mountain, the third-highest peak in California behind Mount Whitney and its High Sierra neighbor Mount Williamson.

The best time to visit the ancient pines is June through October. Summertime is more like springtime in the White Mountains. Patches of snow linger in shady crevices. Wildflowers such as lupine and Indian paintbrush do not bloom until August, or even September.

Allow yourself at least half a day to hike both Discovery and Methuselah trails. At Schulman Grove, where the trails begin, is a small visitor center and some interpretive displays. With the displays and pamphlets, you can learn more about the emerging science of dendrochronology, from Leonardo da Vinci's discovery of tree-ring dating to modern radiocarbon methodology, than you ever wanted to know. During summer months, naturalists sometimes staff the visitor center and give talks about the bristlecone ecology.

Directions to trailhead: This is one hike where getting there really is half the fun—a most scenic drive.

From Highway 395 in Big Pine (south of Bishop), turn east on Highway 168 (Westgard Pass Road) and drive 13 miles to the signed turnoff for the bristlecone pines. About 5½ miles from the highway, you'll spot Grandview Campground and a few miles later come to a glorious viewpoint. Sierra View lives up to the promise of its name, delivering a panorama of eastern High Sierra peaks.

At the end of the paved road is Schulman Grove, where there's plenty of parking. Both Discovery and Methuselah trails are well signed.

Inyo Mountains Wilderness
Lonesome Miner Trail

Terrain: Rugged west side of Inyo Mountains.
Highlights: Historic miners' route; grand Saline Valley views.
Distance: From Hunter Canyon to tent platforms is 6 miles round-trip with 2,100-foot elevation gain.
Degree of difficulty: Moderate to strenuous.

Lonesome Miner Trail is every bit as lonely as its name suggests—an old prospectors' route through some of the most rugged and remote backcountry in California.

No doubt most of the many old miners' trails in the Inyo Mountains could be categorized as lonesome, but this particular path was named by volunteer trail builders and the Bureau of Land Management, who worked very hard to discover—and uncover—the trail. It traverses the Inyo Mountain Wilderness, established in 1994.

Forty-mile-long Lonesome Miner Trail, strenuous and difficult to follow, extends from Hunter Canyon in the Saline Valley to Reward Canyon in the Owens Valley. It's a patchwork of historic trails built by miners from 1867 to 1941. The path descends into and climbs out of several steep canyons on the east side of the Inyo Mountains and passes several historic mining sites. Vistas from the trail's high points include the High Sierra and Death Valley National Park.

One of the easier to follow and more accessible stretches of trail, and a good introduction to the east side of the Inyo Mountains, is the section through Hunter Canyon, sometimes called the Hunter Canyon Trail. A good destination for a day hike is what I've called Miners Camp, where prospectors hewed a 20-by-80-foot campsite out of a rock ledge, then built three wooden tent platforms. The ledge and platforms make an intriguing picnic site or campsite and offer a commanding view of the Saline Valley below.

Directions to trailhead: From Highway 190, about 35 miles east of Lone Pine, turn north on Saline Valley Road and drive 38 miles to Saline Valley Marsh. A ½-mile north of the entrance to this historic site, turn west and drive a mile to road's end and the signed trailhead for Hunter Canyon Trail.

The walk: From the old mine equipment in Little Hunter Canyon, the path follows the creek bed past some mesquite thickets up the canyon for ¼-mile. The trail then leaves the canyon, switchbacking up to the ridge on the south side.

The ridge route continues ascending, offering grand views eastward of Saline Valley, the Last Chance Range, and the northwestern reaches of Death Valley National Park. Enjoy the excellent view from Miners Camp as well.

From Miners Camp, Lonesome Miner Trail continues climbing more than 3,000 feet in elevation, steeply up the ridge. After topping the ridge, the path descends steeply to Bighorn Spring, another 3 miles or so from the trailhead.

Fossil Falls

Fossil Falls Trail

Terrain: Lava cascade.
Highlights: Unique volcanic geology.
Distance: ½-mile round-trip.
Degree of difficulty: Easy.

Some 20,000 years ago, molten lava flowed into the bed of the Owens River. The river waters have since sculpted and polished the lava rock into some stunning forms—among them the lava cascade known as Fossil Falls.

At the very least, a visitor can't help but be impressed by the two mighty forces—volcanism and running water—that created and shaped the scenery in this corner of the West Mojave.

The second sterling example of volcanism in the vicinity is the red cinder cone just north of the lava flow. Red Hill, as the locals call it, is quarried for its cinders, which are used for roads, running tracks, and decoration.

Archaeologists have found evidence of Native American habitation in the Fossil Falls area dating from 4000 B.C. to the 19th century. Rock rings supported brush-and-tule shelters that served the Shoshone.

Splotches of orange paint on the rocks help you stay on the short trail to Fossil Falls, where the cliffs are quite impressive. Be very careful. Rock climbers and local search-and-rescue teams practice their skills at Fossil Falls.

Directions to trailhead: From Highway 14, 20 miles north of its junction with Highway 395 (and 3 miles north of the all-but-abandoned hamlet of Little Lake), turn east on signed Cinder Road. Travel ½-mile on the road, which soon turns from pavement to gravel, to the BLM-signed turnoff on your right for Fossil Falls. Follow this gravel road south, then east, for 1½ miles to a parking lot and day-use area.

Trona Pinnacles

Trona Trail

> **Terrain:** Weird maze of tufa (calcium carbonate) monoliths.
> **Highlights:** Unforgettable science-fiction landscape.
> **Distance:** A mile or so round-trip.
> **Degree of difficulty:** Easy.
> **Precautions:** Tufa is as sharp as coral.

On the way to Death Valley, off a road to nowhere, are the Trona Pinnacles, one of the most unusual sights in the Mojave Desert. Five hundred tufa towers, many more than 100 feet high, rise from Searles Dry Lake basin.

From a distance, the pinnacles appear to be the ruins of some ancient, otherworldly civilization. Trekkies and movie buffs will recognize the Trona Pinnacles as one of the out-of-this-world locations in the Star Trek adventure *The Final Frontier.*

Scientists believe the tufa (calcium carbonate) rock formations developed some 10,000 to 100,000 years ago when Searles Lake was a substantial body of water fed by rainfall and by runoff from retreating Sierra Nevada glaciers. The pinnacles formed underwater in the mineral-rich lake. Highly concentrated calcium carbonate brine bonded with algae to make reeflike formations of hollow tubes, then the spires that we see exposed today. The tufa formations are similar to the ones rising above Mono Lake.

The pinnacles are spread over a 4-mile-long, 3-mile-wide area, but the main concentration of spires can be reached by an easy walk from the parking area. Wander at will from tufa tower to tufa tower as far as time and imagination permit. Sturdy footwear is required on this walk; tufa cuts like coral.

Directions to trailhead: From Highway 395, exit on Highway 178 (which begins as Ridgecrest Road, then continues as Trona Road). From the town of Ridgecrest, it's 11 miles east to Pinnacles Road. Turn right on Pinnacles Road (paved for ¼-mile, rutted dirt thereafter) and travel 7 miles to the pinnacles.

Red Rock Canyon State Park
Hagen, Red Cliffs Trails

Terrain: Steep-walled gorges, badlands of El Paso Mountains.
Highlights: Colorful cliffs, natural preserves.
Distance: 1 to 2 miles round-trip.
Degree of difficulty: Easy to moderate.
Precautions: Inquire about dirt road conditions.

The view of Red Rock Canyon may very well seem like déjà vu. Cliffs and canyons in these parts have appeared in the background of many a Western movie.

A black-and-white movie of Red Rock Canyon would be dramatic: shadow and light playing over the canyon walls. Technicolor, however, might more vividly capture the aptly named red rock, along with the chocolate brown, black, white, and pink hues of the pleated cliffs.

This moviemaker's—and hiker's—dream location is about 125 miles north of Los Angeles off Highway 14 at Red Rock Canyon State Park. The park is situated at a biologic crossroads between the Mojave Desert to the south and the High Sierra to the northwest. Red Rock is also at a geologic crossroads between the Mojave and Great Basin deserts, having formations common to each.

The dramatic, eroded sedimentary cliffs we see today accumulated in a lake bed during Miocene times, some 10 million years ago. The soft sandstone rock is capped by a hard lava cap rock, which protects the colorful formations and slows down their erosion.

Preserved in the cliffs is a fossil record fascinating to paleontologists. Millions of years ago, Red Rock Canyon was a freshwater lake, ringed by oak and even palm trees, where saber-toothed cats, elephants, and rhinoceroses roamed.

The first human inhabitants, the Kawai'isu, came to the Red Rock Canyon area more than 10,000 years ago.

Gold fever in the 1890s prompted exploration of almost all the canyons in the El Paso Mountains. During this era, Rudolph Hagen acquired much land in the Red Rock area. He named the little mining community and stage stop Ricardo after his son Richard. The Ricardo Ranger Station is located at the site of the once-thriving hamlet.

Red Rock Canyon became a state recreation area in 1969; when it became obvious that off-road vehicles were damaging the hills and canyons, Red Rock was upgraded to a park in 1982.

The best places to hike are in the park's two preserves, which are closed to vehicles. You'll find some trails to hike, but this park lends itself to improvisation.

The park nature trail, a ¾-mile path, tells the geologic story of the area and points out typical desert flora. It's keyed to an interpretive pamphlet available at the trailhead. Join the nature trail at the south end of the park campground.

Hagen Canyon Natural Preserve is a striking badlands, the dramatic cliffs capped by a layer of dark basalt. A primitive 1-mile loop trail explores the canyon.

Red Cliffs Natural Preserve protects the 300-foot sandstone cliffs east of Highway 14. No developed trail exists, but hikers can enjoy a mile or so of cross-country travel through the preserve.

Directions to trailhead: Red Rock Canyon State Park is 25 miles north of the town of Mojave off Highway 14. Turn northwest off 14 onto the signed road for the park campground. Follow this road a short mile to Ricardo Ranger Station. The station has a small visitor center with nature exhibits. Check with rangers about the condition of the many dirt roads that explore the park and surrounding desert. Guided nature walks are sometimes available on weekends during the spring and fall months.

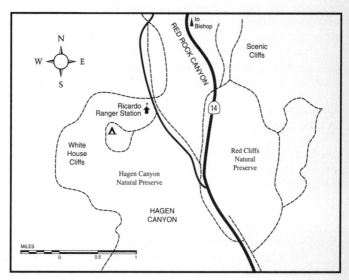

Desert Tortoise Natural Area

Main Loop Trail, Discovery Trail

Terrain: Creosote bush–covered flatlands.
Highlights: California's state reptile in native habitat; showy desert wildflowers.
Distance: ½-mile to 5 miles round-trip.
Degree of difficulty: Easy.
Precautions: Do not touch the tortoises; under no circumstances, release a pet or captive tortoise in the reserve.

Everything a desert tortoise is—patient, quiet, slow, a homebody—we fast-paced urbanites are not. Perhaps, then, that's why we Californians so admire our official state reptile.

One of the best places to glimpse a *Gopherus agassizi* is at the Desert Tortoise Natural Area in the West Mojave Desert near California City. March through mid-June is the best time to see a tortoise, and spring is the prime time to view the desert wildflowers blooming around their burrows.

Ancestors of the present-day desert tortoise roamed the earth with dinosaurs and, until recently, managed to adapt to changing environmental conditions. Then came grazing animals that squashed them and collapsed their burrows, and off-road vehicles that did likewise, as well as residential and commercial development that obliterated their habitat. Tortoises have been illegally collected, shot at in perverse fun, even sold as dog food in Los Angeles during the 1890s.

Once upon a time, the western Mojave Desert supported as many as 2,000 tortoises per square mile. Today the tortoise population is a fraction of that, and the creature is considered a "threatened" species by state and federal governments.

One of the densest remaining populations of tortoises can be found in the 21,000-acre Desert Tortoise Natural Area set aside 20 years ago by conservation groups and the Bureau of Land Management to give the venerable reptiles a fighting chance for survival. The tortoises inside their fenced preserve seem to be doing better than their fellows out in the open desert, though the preserve population has suffered from diseases brought in by unthinking people who release captive tortoises in the natural area. As a result, the tortoises become afflicted with a difficult-to-cure upper respiratory condition that spreads rapidly through the population.

In springtime, the tortoises emerge from their burrows to feed. They stay very close to the burrows, wandering off only for a little eating, basking, or mating. They grow to 14 inches long and live a very slow 50 to 100 years.

When I visited the preserve recently, I had the passing thought that somewhere out in the Mojave is an old tortoise that has witnessed both a stagecoach passing and the space shuttle landing.

The first stop for visitors should be the colorfully painted motor home that is the Desert Tortoise Natural Area headquarters during the March–June "tortoise season." Out front are a couple of exhibits, some free information sheets, and tortoise T-shirts for sale.

Several trails crisscross the Desert Tortoise Natural Area. *Main Loop Trail* makes a short circle from the parking area and connects to Plant Trail and Animal Trail, self-guided nature walks with interpretive pamphlets that explain, respectively, the local flora and fauna.

More ambitious is the 1⅕-mile *Discovery Loop Trail,* which follows strategically placed brown posts emblazoned with a hiker's logo across the open desert. In the shelter of the spreading creosote bushes are phacelia, fiddleneck, goldfields, and evening snow. Near headquarters is the stunning desert candle.

Look for tortoise burrows—and tortoises—near the creosote bushes. Your best chance for spotting a tortoise is in the morning hours and in the late afternoon. You are more likely to see one away from the nature trails than right next to the paths. Ask the naturalist, on duty during the spring visitors season, for help in locating a tortoise.

Directions to trailhead: From Highway 14 (Antelope Valley Freeway), 5 miles north of the town of Mojave, exit on California City Boulevard. Drive some 10 miles east (through California City). Turn left (northeast) on Twenty Mule Team Parkway and drive 1⅗ miles to Randsburg-Mojave Road. Turn left at this junction, where you'll find a shaded picnic area and information panels about the desert tortoise. Follow the dirt road (usually in good shape, but almost impassable after a hard rain) 4½ miles to the Desert Tortoise Natural Area parking lot.

Antelope Valley California Poppy Reserve

Antelope Loop Trail

Terrain: Gentle hills of Antelope Valley.
Highlights: California's state flower in magnificent, seasonal bloom.
Distance: From visitor center to Antelope Butte Vista Point is 2½ miles round-trip with 300-foot elevation gain.
Degree of difficulty: Easy to moderate.

The California poppy blooms on many a grassy slope in the Southland, but only in the Antelope Valley does the showy flower blanket whole hillsides in such brilliant orange sheets. Surely the finest concentration of California's state flower (during a good wildflower year) is preserved at the Antelope Valley California Poppy Reserve in the Mojave Desert west of Lancaster.

The poppy is the star of the flower show, which includes a supporting cast of fiddlenecks, creamcups, tidytips, and goldfields. March through Memorial Day is the time to saunter through this wondrous display of desert wildflowers.

The poppy has always been recognized as something special. Early Spanish Californians called it *dormidera,* "the drowsy one," because the petals curl up at night. They fashioned a hair tonic/restorer by frying the blossoms in olive oil and adding perfume.

At the reserve, you can pick up a map at the Jane S. Pineiro Interpretive Center, named for the painter who was instrumental in setting aside an area where California's state flower could be preserved for future generations to admire. Some of Pineiro's watercolors are displayed at the center, which also has wildflower interpretive displays and a slide show.

Built into the side of a hill, the center boasts an award-winning solar design, windmill power, and "natural air conditioning."

Antelope Loop Trail, like the other trails in the reserve, is easy walking and suitable for the whole family. Seven miles of gentle trails crisscross the 1,760-acre reserve; many hikers take every trail in the park without getting too tired.

Directions to trailhead: From the Antelope Valley Freeway (Highway 14) in Lancaster, exit on Avenue I and drive west 15 miles. Avenue I becomes Lancaster Road a few miles before the Poppy Reserve. The reserve is open from 9:00 A.M. to 4:00 P.M. daily. There is a state park day-use fee.

Spring wildflower displays are always unpredictable. To check what's blooming where, call the park at (805) 724–1180 before making the trip.

The walk: Begin on the signed Antelope Loop Trail to the left of the visitor center. The trail passes through an orange sea of poppies and fiddlenecks, then climbs briefly to Kitanemuk Vista Point, ¾-mile from the visitor center. Atop Vista Point are those flowery symbols of faithfulness and friendship, forget-me-nots, and an unforgettable view of the Mojave Desert and the snow-covered Tehachapis.

After enjoying the view, continue to Antelope Butte Vista Point, where another lookout offers fine desert panoramas. From here, join the south loop of the Antelope Loop Trail and return to the visitor center.

After you've circled the "upper west side" of the Poppy Reserve, you may wish to extend your hike by joining the Poppy Loop Trail and exploring the "lower east side."

Saddleback Butte State Park
Saddleback Butte Trail

> **Terrain:** Granite mountain above Antelope Valley.
> **Highlights:** Joshua tree woodland, desert vistas.
> **Distance:** From campground to Saddleback Peak is 4 miles round-trip with 1,000-foot elevation gain.
> **Degree of difficulty:** Moderate.

Rarely visited Saddleback Butte State Park, located on the eastern fringe of Antelope Valley, offers an easily reached but out-of-the-way destination for a day hike.

This is high-desert country, a land of creosote bushes and Joshua trees. The park, located 75 miles north of Los Angeles, takes the name of its most prominent feature—3,651-foot Saddleback Butte, a granite mountaintop that stands head and shoulders above Antelope Valley.

The spartan country around the butte once supported thousands of pronghorn antelope—hence the name Antelope Valley—and the numerous Native American tribes who hunted them. The antelopes are all gone now, victims to hunting and encroaching civilization. By interrupting the antelopes' migration, Southern Pacific railroad tracks also doomed the animals; the antelope could easily cross the tracks, but instinct prevented them from doing this, and they soon perished from exposure to harsh winters and the shrinkage of their habitat.

Today's park visitor may glimpse several other animals native to Antelope Valley, including coyotes, jackrabbits, lizards, and the Antelope ground squirrel. Some fortunate hikers may even witness the unhurried progress of a desert tortoise.

Before you hike to the top of the butte, you may wish to walk the short nature trail near the park entrance. It's a good introduction to the Joshua tree and other plant life found in this corner of the desert.

Guided walks are sometimes conducted along Joshua Trail during autumn and spring months on Sunday mornings. Check at the visitor center for more information.

The trail to the boulder-strewn summit of Saddleback Peak takes a straight-line course, with most of the elevation gain occurring in the last ½-mile. Atop the peak, the hiker is rewarded with far-reaching desert views.

Directions to trailhead: From Highway 14 (Antelope Valley Freeway) in Lancaster, take the Twentieth Street exit. Head north on Twentieth and turn east (right) on Avenue J. Drive about 18 miles, past barren land and farmland, to Saddleback Butte State Park. Follow the dirt park road to the campground, where the trail begins. Park near the trail sign. There is a state park day-use fee.

The walk: The signed trail heads straight for the saddle. The soft, sandy track, marked with yellow posts (this may be the best-marked trail in the state park system), leads through an impressive Joshua tree woodland.

With the exception of pathfinder John C. Frémont, who called it "the most repulsive tree in the vegetable kingdom," most California travelers have found the Joshua tree to be quite picturesque. Mormon pioneers thought that the tree's outstretched limbs resembled the prophet Joshua pointing to the promised land.

After 1½ miles, the trail begins to switchback steeply up the rocky slope of the butte. An invigorating climb brings you to the saddle of Saddleback Butte. To reach Saddleback Peak, follow the steep left-ward trail to the summit.

From the top, you can look south to the San Gabriel Mountains. You may be able to spot Mount Baldy, dominating the eastern end of the range. Keen eyes will discern the California Aqueduct at the base of the mountains; it carries water to the Southland from the Sacramento Delta. To the east is the vast Mojave Desert; to the north is Edwards Air Force Base. To the west are the cities of Lancaster and Palmdale and farther west, the rugged Tehachapi Mountains.

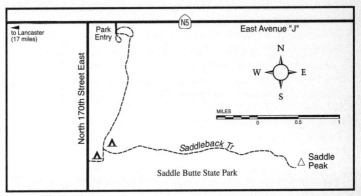

Vasquez Rocks

Geology, Pacific Crest Trails

Terrain: Tilted sandstone outcrops, sagebrush- and juniper-covered hills.
Highlights: Breathtaking geological formations, rock climbing.
Distance: 1 to 3 miles round-trip.
Degree of difficulty: Easy.

Chances are you've seen the rocks on TV and the big screen many times—from old Westerns to modern science-fiction films. And you've probably noticed Vasquez Rocks while motoring along the Antelope Valley Freeway; the famed formations are but a couple of miles from Highway 14.

But the best place to see the Southland's most famous geological silhouette is Vasquez Rocks County Park Natural Area in Agua Dulce. Hiking trails circle the rocks, which are not only enjoyable to view but fun to climb upon.

Through a camera lens, and from a distance, the rocks look insurmountable; actually, they're rather easy to climb. The rocks are only 100–150 feet high, and you can find safe and mellow routes to the top of the sandstone outcrops.

The rocks themselves are tilted and worn sandstone, the result of years of earthquake action and erosion by the elements. The big beds of sedimentary rock known as the Mint Canyon Formation were laid down some 8 to 15 million years ago. The Vasquez Rocks Formation is composed of coarser, redder layers underneath.

Tataviam Indians occupied the area until the late 18th century, when their culture was overwhelmed and eventually extinguished by the soldiers, settlers, and missionaries of the San Fernando Mission.

During the 1850s and 1860s, notorious highwayman Tiburcio Vasquez used the rocks and canyons as a hideout from the Los Angeles lawmen who were pursuing him. Even before he was hanged for his crimes in 1875, the area was known as Vasquez Rocks.

The trail system at Vasquez Rocks is a bit informal. Because of the open nature of the terrain, hikers can—and do—tend to wander where their rock fancy takes them. If you remember that the park entrance/office is more or less to the north and that Antelope Valley Freeway is to the south, you'll stay fairly well oriented.

One of my favorite routes, a clockwise tour of 3 miles or so, is described below; however, part of the fun of Vasquez Rocks is going your own way.

Directions to trailhead: From the Antelope Valley Freeway (Highway 14), a few miles northeast of the outskirts of Canyon Country, exit on Agua Dulce Road. Drive north 1½ miles. Agua Dulce Road swings west and you join Escondido Canyon Road, proceeding ¼-mile to the signed Vasquez Rocks County Park entrance on your right. You can park just inside the entrance at the small parking area near the park office, or continue to the main lot near the largest of the rock formations.

The walk: Begin at the signed trailhead for Geology Trail just across the park road from the parking lot. (Pick up an interpretive brochure, as well as a trail map, from the office.) Soon after you begin your trailside study of strata, Geology Trail intersects Pacific Crest Trail and you'll head right.

The mile-long stretch of Pacific Crest Trail through the park is part of a segment that connects the San Gabriel Mountains to the south with the Sierra Pelona area of Angeles National Forest to the north. The path parallels the park road. To your left are a few scattered residences and the open desert beyond; to your right are some of the most famous of the Vasquez Rocks.

Pacific Crest Trail joins a dirt road at the edge of the picnic area and continues west atop the north wall of Escondido Canyon. Very few park visitors, it seems, hike here, though the rock formations are stunning and a seasonal creek flows through the canyon. Only the annoying hum of the nearby Antelope Valley Freeway disturbs the natural beauty.

You can cross the creek with the Pacific Crest Trail, double back along the other side of Escondido Canyon, and continue your exploration of the little-known southern part of the park. But to continue to the main rock formations, stay west with the dirt road and you'll soon reach a junction with the park's horse trail. You can take this trail if you wish or continue a short distance farther and join the foot trail.

The Vasquez Rocks area is a transition zone between mountain and desert environments. Yucca, buckwheat, sage, and California juniper are among the plants you'll pass en route.

The footpath drops northwestward, then heads east to visit the most dramatic of the Vasquez Rocks.

67

Devil's Punchbowl

Devil's Punchbowl Loop Trail

> **Terrain:** Beige-colored tilted sandstone formations.
> **Highlights:** Marvelous maze in earthquake country.
> **Distance:** 1-mile loop from visitor center.
> **Degree of difficulty:** Easy.

Devil's Punchbowl Loop Trail is an ideal, family-friendly introduction to a strange wonderland of rock that sits astride the San Andreas Fault. Along with earthquakes, the erosive forces of wind and water have carved the sharply angled sandstone formations.

Devil's Punchbowl itself may have been the work of the devil, or more likely, it is a deep canyon cut by streams running out of the San Gabriel Mountains. Over millions of years, the streams tore at the sedimentary rock and eroded the steep and cockeyed rock layers of the Punchbowl formation. Originally horizontal, these layers of siltstone and sandstone were folded into a syncline (U-shaped fold) by the pinching action of earthly forces.

A ³⁄₁₀-mile-long nature trail, Pinyon Pathway, introduces visitors to park geology and plant life, and the 1-mile loop trail offers grand

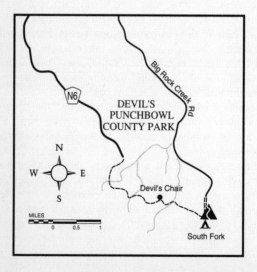

views of the Punchbowl. A picnic area is perched on the rim of the Punchbowl.

The more intrepid may wish to explore lower Punchbowl Canyon, located below Devil's Punchbowl Loop Trail. Access this canyon from Big Rock Creek Road.

Directions to trailhead: From Highway 138 on the east edge of Pearblossom, exit on County Road N–6 (Longview Road) and proceed south 7½ miles to the entrance of Devil's Punchbowl Natural Area Park.

Enjoy the Punchbowl's wonderland of rocks, an easy adventure for the whole family.

Devil's Chair

Punchbowl Trail

Terrain: Huge, tilted slabs of sandstone.
Highlights: Close-up look at earthquake-twisted landscape.
Distance: From South Fork Campground to Devil's Chair is
6 miles round-trip with 1,000-foot elevation gain; to park
headquarters is 12 miles round-trip.
Degree of difficulty: Moderate.

California has many faults, and the mightiest is the San Andreas. Nowhere is the presence of this fault more obvious than in Devil's Punchbowl County Park. The dun-colored rocks have been tilted every which way and weathered by wind and rain. They are a bizarre sight to behold.

Punchbowl Trail takes you into the devil's domain, a satanically landscaped rock garden on the desert side of the San Gabriel Mountains. The trip offers views of the Punchbowl and San Jacinto faults—part of what seismologists call the San Andreas Rift Zone. If you're superstitious, you'll want to carry a good-luck charm in your day pack when you hike to the monstrous mass of white rock known as the Devil's Chair.

Winter is a fine time to visit the Punchbowl. Winds scour the desert clean, and from the Devil's Chair you can get superb views of this land, as well as the seemingly infinite sandscape of the Mojave.

Note that the 6-mile Punchbowl Trail may be hiked from two directions. For aesthetic and logistical reasons, I prefer the route from the Forest Service's South Fork Campground to Devil's Chair.

The leg-weary or families with small children may wish to proceed directly to Devil's Punchbowl County Park. A ⅓-mile nature trail, Pinyon Pathway, introduces visitors to park geology and plant life, and a 1-mile loop trail offers grand views of the Punchbowl.

Directions to trailhead: From Pearblossom Highway (Highway 138) in Pearblossom, turn south onto Longview Road, then briefly left on Fort Tejon Road and right on Valyermo Road. Continue 3 miles to Big Rock Creek Road. Two and a half miles past this junction, turn right on a signed dirt road to South Fork Campground and proceed 1 mile to the special day-use/hikers' parking lot below the campground. The road is suitable for passenger cars but, occasionally, Big Rock Creek may be too high for a low-slung car to ford; you may have to walk an extra mile to the trailhead. The signed trail departs from the parking area.

If you want to go directly to Devil's Punchbowl County Park, turn south on County Road N–6 from Highway 138 in Pearblossom and follow it to the county park. Punchbowl Trail begins near the picnic area.

The walk: From the parking area below South Fork Campground, join the signed trail. Almost immediately, you'll reach a junction. (Steep South Fork Trail ascends the canyon cut by the south fork of Big Rock Creek up to the Angeles Crest Highway at Islip Saddle.)

Stay on Punchbowl Trail and boulder-hop across the creek. If your imagination has already run away with you, perhaps the mythological Charon the Ferryman (who conveyed the dead to Hades over the river Styx) will carry you across this watercourse.

The trail climbs through manzanita and heat-stunted pinyon pine to a saddle where there's a view of the park and its faults. Descend from the saddle, down chaparral-covered slopes and over to Holcomb Canyon. Along the way, notice the strange dovetailing of three plant communities: yucca-covered hills, oak woodland, and juniper and piney woods.

You may wish to take a break near Holcomb Creek crossing. Oaks and big-cone spruces shade the creek.

From Holcomb Creek, the trail ascends steeply up another ridge through a pinyon pine forest to the Devil's Chair. From a distance, those with fanciful imaginations can picture the devil himself ruling over this kingdom of fractured rock. Below the chair, there's an awesome panorama of the Punchbowl and its jumbled sedimentary strata. The somersaulted sandstone formation resembles pulled taffy. If you look west to the canyon wall, you can see the vertical crush zone of the fault, marked by white rocks.

While visiting the Devil's Chair, stay behind the protective fence; people have taken a plunge into the Punchbowl. Return to the trailhead the way you came or continue on the Punchbowl Trail to county park headquarters.

Above Devil's Chair, the trail contours west and offers close-up views of the Punchbowl. A mile-and-a-half from the Chair, your route crosses Punchbowl Creek, briefly joins a dirt road, then bears right on the trail leading to the Punchbowl parking area.

Views that extend for miles—just one of the attractions of Mojave National Preserve.

3. Mojave National Preserve

As you hike to the top of Kelso Dunes you might just find that the dunes sha-boom-sha-boom-sha-boom for you. Geologists speculate that the extreme dryness of the East Mojave Desert, combined with the wind-polished, rounded nature of the individual sand grains, has something to do with their musical ability.

Except for the sha-booming, the Kelso Dunes are absolutely quiet. Often, hikers find they have a 45-square-mile formation of magnificently sculpted sand, the most extensive dune field in the West, all to themselves.

Two decades of park politicking finally ended in October 1994 when Congress passed a desert protection bill sponsored by Senator Dianne Feinstein. The California Desert Protection Act transferred the East Mojave National Scenic Area, administered by the U.S. Bureau of Land Management, to the National Park Service and established the new Mojave National Preserve. The Mojave's elevated national profile has not yet attracted hordes of sightseers.

To many travelers, the East Mojave is that vast, bleak, interminable stretch of desert to be crossed as quickly as possible while driving Interstate 15 from Barstow to Las Vegas. Few realize that I–15 is the northern boundary of what desert rats have long called "the Crown Jewel of the California Desert," and what is now Mojave National Preserve. Some 17 million people live less than a 4 hour's drive from the East Mojave, but few city dwellers can locate this desert land on the map, and even fewer visit it.

Although virtually unknown, Mojave National Preserve is quite accessible; it's bounded north and south by two major interstates, I–15 and I–40, and on the east by U.S. Highway 95. Just south of I–40 is one of the longest remaining stretches of old Route 66. Still, the area delimited by these three highways has long been dubbed "The Lonesome Triangle" and will probably keep this nickname for many years to come.

With few campgrounds and even fewer motels, without a visitor center or even a decent map, this land is a hard one to get to know—but an easy one to get to like: 1.4 million acres that include such wonders as canyons sculpted by the Mojave River, the vast caves of Mitchell Caverns, and the world's largest Joshua tree forest. Mojave National Preserve offers the chance to relive history by hiking traditional paths to Fort Piute and Hole-in-the-Wall and by driving the old Mojave Road and fabled Route 66. In the new preserve is a wonderful concentration of mining history, backroads and foot-paths, tabletop mesas, cinder cones, and a dozen mountain ranges. This diversity, everything that makes a desert a desert, draws us to experience its silent places. It's a call of the wild that can't be heard, only felt and experienced.

The view from atop the Kelso Dunes is grand: the Kelso Mountains to the north, the Bristol Mountains to the southwest, the Granite Mountains to the south, the Providence Mountains to the east. Everywhere are mountain ranges, small and large, from the jagged, red, spirelike Castle Peaks to the flat-topped Table Mountain. In fact, despite evidence to the contrary—most notably the stunning Kelso Dunes—the East Mojave is really a desert of mountains, not sand.

From the old Kelso Train Depot, lonesome backroads lead toward Cima Dome, a 75-square-mile chunk of uplifted volcanic rock. A geological rarity, Cima has been called the most symmetrical natural dome in the United States. Another distinctive feature of the dome is its handsome rock outcroppings—the same type found in Joshua Tree National Park to the south. Rock climbers, rock scramblers, and hikers love Cima's rock show.

On and around Cima Dome is the world's largest and densest Joshua tree forest. Botanists say Cima's Joshuas are more symmetrical than their cousins elsewhere in the Mojave, though to me every tree looks different, every one a rugged individualist with branches that seem like handfuls of daggers.

Hole-in-the-Wall and Mid Hills are the centerpieces of Mojave National Preserve. Both locales offer diverse desert scenery, fine campgrounds, and the feeling of being in the middle of nowhere—though, in fact, they are located right in the middle of the preserve.

Linking Mid Hills to Hole-in-the-Wall is an 8-mile trail, my favorite hike in the East Mojave; nearby is the preserve's best drive. In 1989 Wildhorse Canyon Road, which loops from Mid Hills Campground to Hole-in-the-Wall Campground, was declared the nation's first official "Back Country Byway," an honor bestowed upon America's most scenic backroads.

Hole-in-the-Wall is the kind of place Butch Cassidy and the Sundance Kid would choose as a hideout. Geologists call this twisted maze of red rock rhyolite, a kind of lava that existed as hot liquid far below the earth's surface, then crystallized. A series of iron rings aids descent into Hole-in-the-Wall; they're not particularly difficult for those who are reasonably agile and take their time.

Kelso Dunes, the Joshua trees, Hole-in-the-Wall, and Mid Hills—the heart of the new preserve—can be viewed in a weekend. But you'll need a week just to see all the major sights, and maybe a life-time to really get to know the East Mojave. Return for a meander through a "botanical island," the pinyon pine and juniper woodland in Caruthers Canyon; tour Ivanpah Valley, which supports the largest desert tortoise population in the California desert, and see if you can spot one of the elusive creatures; climb atop enormous volcanic cinder cones, then with flashlights crawl through narrow lava tubes. Return to explore the ruins of Fort Piute: wonder about the lonely life of the soldiers stationed there; marvel at the ruts carved into rock by the wheels of pioneer wagon trains; guess at the meaning of the petroglyphs left behind by the Native Americans who roamed this land long ago.

Mojave National Preserve is a worthy addition to the national park system and a great place to take a hike.

Life persists in the unlikeliest places.

Rainbow Basin

Owl Canyon Trail

> **Terrain:** Colorful hills.
> **Highlights:** Multicolored rock amphitheater.
> **Distance:** From Owl Canyon Campground to Velvet Peak
> is 5 miles round-trip with 500-foot elevation gain.
> **Degree of difficulty:** Moderate.

The "National Natural Landmark" designation on the map is a tip-off, but nothing can prepare you for the sight of the spectacular series of colorful hills that make up Rainbow Basin. Pink, white, orange, brown, red, black, and green sediments form the basin's rainbow-colored walls.

Rainbow Basin is administered by the Bureau of Land Management. It's located just north of I–15 in Barstow, and just outside Mojave National Preserve. It is, to say the least, extremely scenic. This geologically fascinating destination in the Calico Mountains is ideal for on-foot exploration.

Some 15 million years ago, grasslands filled Rainbow Basin, which was populated by saber-toothed tigers, mastodons, camels,

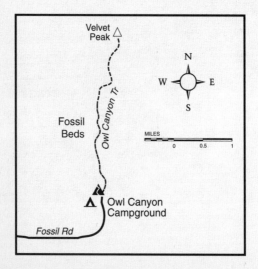

three-toed horses, and even rhinoceroses. Their fossil remains are encased in sedimentary rock that once formed a lake bed. As a result of intense geologic activity over the millennia, what was once at the bottom of the lake is now a series of folded, faulted, colorful hills.

Owl Canyon is one of three moderate hikes in Rainbow Basin. This canyon takes its name from the barn owls who live there. To tackle Owl Canyon Trail, hikers need to be reasonably agile, because getting through the canyon means scrambling over some boulders.

You could spend a pleasant weekend camping and hiking in Rainbow Basin. Stationed at Owl Canyon Campground is a campground host, who can provide hiking and touring tips.

Directions to trailhead: Follow Interstate 15 to Barstow, then join Highway 58 to Fort Irwin Road, following it 5 miles. Turn west on dirt Fossil Road and proceed 3 miles to Owl Canyon Campground. The trail begins at the north end of the campground.

The walk: Follow the marked trail into Owl Canyon. A ½-mile up-canyon look for a small cave on your right.

Sandstone and siltstone, shale, and volcanic debris are among the exposed rocks visible to the hiker. The geologic formations en route are not only rainbow-colored but dramatic in shape. Particularly evident are the massive downfolds that geologists call synclines.

The canyon narrows for a time, then opens up at its end into a multicolored amphitheater. Velvet Peak is the high spot above the rocky bowl. Experienced hikers can scramble up the bowl's rocky ridges for fine views of Rainbow Basin and the vast East Mojave Desert.

Afton Canyon

Afton Canyon Trail

Terrain: Deep canyon of Mojave River.
Highlights: "Grand Canyon of the Mojave."
Distance: From Afton Campground to Pyramid Canyon is 3
 miles round-trip; to side canyons is 6½ miles round-trip.
Degree of difficulty: Moderate.

Afton Canyon is often called the Grand Canyon of the Mojave.
High praise indeed, but then it's a very special place, a geological
wonderland sculpted by the Mojave River.

The Bureau of Land Management is in the process of rehabilitat-
ing the canyon. Decades of off-road vehicle use tore up the ancient
Mojave riverbed and gouged the surrounding hills. Overgrazing led
to the invasion of opportunistic plants such as the tamarisk that
suck up scarce water. The BLM has rerouted off-road vehicles out
of the canyon floor, eliminated grazing, and begun to restore the native plant community.

Long ago, Afton Canyon was cut by outlet-flow from a once-
large body of water that geologists call Lake Mannix. Some 15,000
to 75,000 years ago, during a hot and much more humid period,
wildlife abounded around the lake, which was shallow but covered
about 200 square miles. Turtles, shellfish, camels, antelope, and
flocks of pink flamingos gathered at the lake.

The Mojave River, during these wetter times, must have been a
stream of considerable size. Even in today's arid climate, the Mojave manages to flow either below ground or above for 145 miles
across the desert.

The (relatively) well watered Mojave River Valley has always
served as a route of travel. During prehistoric times, Native Americans traveled the Mojave Trail from the California coast to the Colorado River. De Anza's 1776 expedition passed through Afton
Canyon on its way to Mission San Gabriel.

A half-century later, Jedediah Smith followed the Mojave and
after getting a bit exasperated with the river's habit of disappear-
ing underground for long stretches, called it, most aptly, "The In-
constant River." Kit Carson took the river route, as did John C.
Frémont, who gave the Mojave its name.

Today, the best view of Afton Canyon and the path of the Mojave River may belong to the crew of the Union Pacific freight train that rumbles through the canyon. An equally fine view is available to hikers. You can explore large Afton Canyon and its many side canyons, including the largest of them, Pyramid Canyon.

Directions to trailhead: From Interstate 15, 32 miles east of Barstow, take the Afton Canyon exit. Travel 3 miles southwest on a good dirt road to Afton Campground. Park at the campground.

The walk: Before you follow the Mojave River through Afton Canyon, you might want to cross it from the campground, under the first set of railroad trestles, and head south through Pyramid Canyon. The largest and deepest of Afton's side canyons, 1½-mile-long Pyramid Canyon is an easy stroll, and a good introduction to the fascinating geology of the area. The grand rock walls, cut away by the once-mighty Mojave, gradually narrow until you reach what appears to be a dead end. Experienced hikers may want to scramble to the top of this "dead end" for a rewarding view of the surrounding desert landscape.

Return to Afton Canyon and follow the river east. You'll notice an intriguing assemblage of desert riparian growth—native cottonwoods and willows, along with invasive tamarisk.

Continue hiking along the canyon's north wall for breathtaking views of water-eroded formations, and to explore the many side canyons. These canyons are, for the most part, indicated by culverts; look for those located at numbers 192.99 and 194.65. A flashlight is useful for finding your way.

Beyond this point the canyon widens and holds less interest for the hiker. Afton Canyon extends a few more miles to a double trestle bridge near Cave Mountain. For a different perspective of the canyon, consider returning by way of the river bottom.

Cima Dome

Teutonia Peak Trail

Terrain: Symmetrical Cima Dome.
Highlights: World's largest Joshua tree forest.
Distance: From the parking area to Cima Dome, Teutonia
Peak, is 4 miles round-trip.
Degree of difficulty: Moderate.

Cima Dome is certainly one of the easiest Mojave National Preserve sights to reach, but when you reach it, you wonder where it went. It's not a geologic formation you can view close-up: the Dome slopes so gently, it's best viewed from a distance. What Gertrude Stein said of Oakland comes to mind: "There's no there there."

Two places to get "the big picture" of Cima Dome are from Mid Hills Campground and from I–15 as you drive southeast of Baker and crest a low rise.

The dome is a mass of once-molten monzonite, a granitelike rock. Over thousands of years it's been extensively eroded and now sprawls over some 75 square miles. It's more than 10 miles in diameter.

Another distinctive feature of the dome is its handsome rock outcroppings—the same type found in Joshua Tree National Park to the south. Rock climbers, rock scramblers, and hikers love Cima's rock show.

The word to remember around Cima Dome is symmetry. A geological rarity, Cima has been called the most symmetrical natural dome in the United States. If you take a look at the area's USGS topographical map and study Cima's near-concentric contour lines, you'll probably agree with this claim.

Symmetry is also a word used in conjunction with the area's other natural attraction: the Joshua tree. Botanists say Cima's Joshuas are more symmetrical than their cousins elsewhere in the Mojave.

Cima's Joshua trees are tall—some more than 25 feet high—and several hundred years old. Collectively, they form the world's largest and densest Joshua tree forest. Here at an elevation of about 4,000 feet this distinct symbol of the Mojave Desert truly thrives. Bring your camera!

This walk travels the famed Joshua tree forest, then visits Cima Dome, which rises 1,500 feet above the surrounding desert playas.

Directions to trailhead: The beginning of the trail is just off Cima Road, a scenic Back Country Byway that stretches 17 miles from the Cima Road exit on Interstate 15 south to Cima. The signed trailhead is about 9 miles from I–15.

The walk: The mellow 2-mile Teutonia Peak Trail meanders through the Joshua tree forest and ascends to a lookout over Cima Dome. From the lookout, it's a ¼-mile scramble over rocks to the top of Teutonia Peak (elevation 5,755 feet).

The path is maintained by the San Gorgonio chapter of the Sierra Club, which has plans to extend it farther over Cima Dome.

Caruthers Canyon

Caruthers Canyon Trail

> **Terrain:** Coastal canyon–like ecosystem in desert.
> **Highlights:** Pinyon pine–juniper woodland.
> **Distance:** From Caruthers Canyon to gold mine is 3 miles round-trip with 400-foot elevation gain.
> **Degree of difficulty:** Easy to moderate.

Botanists call them disjuncts. Bureaucrats call them UPAs (unusual plant assemblages). The more lyrical naturalists among us call them islands on the land.

By whatever name, the isolated communities of pinyon pine and white fir in the New York Mountains of the East Mojave Desert are very special places. Nearly 300 plant species have been counted on the slopes of this range and in its colorfully named canyons—Cottonwood and Caruthers, Butcher Knife and Fourth of July.

Perhaps the most botanically unusual area in the mountains, indeed in the whole Mojave National Preserve, is Caruthers Canyon. A cool, inviting woodland of pinyon pine and juniper stands in marked contrast to the sparsely vegetated sandscape common in other parts of the desert. The conifers are joined by oaks and a variety of coastal chaparral plants, including manzanita, yerba santa, ceanothus, and coffeeberry.

What is a coastal ecosystem doing in the middle of the desert?

Botanists believe that during wetter times such coastal scrub vegetation was widespread. As the climate became more arid, coastal ecosystems were "stranded" atop high and moist slopes. The botanical islands high in the New York Mountains are outposts of Rocky Mountains and coastal California flora.

Caruthers Canyon is a treat for the hiker. An abandoned dirt road leads through a rocky basin and into a historic gold-mining region. Prospectors began digging in the New York Mountains in the 1860s and continued well into the 20th century. At trail's end are a couple of gold-mine shafts.

The canyon's woodland offers great bird-watching. The Western tanager, gray-headed junco, yellow-breasted chat, and many more species are found here. Circling high in the sky are the raptors—golden eagles, prairie falcons, and red-tailed hawks.

Directions to trailhead: From I–40, 28 miles west of Needles and some 117 miles east of Barstow, exit on Mountain Springs Road. You'll pass the tiny town of Goffs (last chance for provisions) and head north 27½ miles on the main road, known variously as Ivanpah-Goffs Road and Ivanpah Road, to New York Mountains Road. (Parts of Ivanpah Road and New York Mountains Road are dirt; they are suitable for passenger cars with good ground clearance.) Turn left (west) on New York Mountains Road. A couple of OX Cattle Ranch buildings stand near this road's intersection with Ivanpah Road. Drive 5½ miles to an unsigned junction with a dirt road and turn north. Proceed 2 miles to a woodland laced with turnouts that serve as unofficial campsites. Leave your car here; farther along, the road dips into a wash and gets very rough.

The walk: From the Caruthers Canyon "campground" follow the main dirt road up the canyon. As you ascend, look behind you for a great view of Table Mountain, the most dominant peak of the central East Mojave.

Handsome boulders line the trail and frame views of the tall peak before you, New York Mountain. The range's 7,532-foot signature peak is crowned with a botanical island of its own—a relict stand of Rocky Mountain white fir.

A ½-mile along, you'll come to a fork in the road. The rightward road climbs ¼-mile to an old mining shack. Take the left fork, dipping in and out of a wash and gaining a great view of the canyon and its castellated walls.

If it has rained recently, you might find some water collected in pools on the rocky canyon bottom. Enjoy the tranquillity of the gold-mine area, but don't stray into the dark and dangerous shafts.

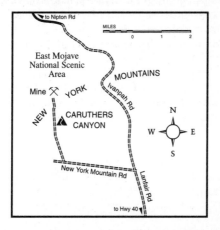

Piute Canyon

Piute Canyon Trail

> **Terrain:** Piute Creek and gorge.
> **Highlights:** Historic fort, oasislike creek.
> **Distance:** 5 miles round-trip with 600-foot elevation gain.
> **Degree of difficulty:** Moderate.

In 1865 a visitor described Fort Piute as "a Godforsaken place—the meanest I ever saw for a military station." It's doubtful that many would disagree; however, the ruins of the fort, along with pretty Piute Valley and Piute Creek, add up to an intriguing, way-off-the-beaten-path tour for the adventurous.

Fort Piute, located east of Lanfair Valley, at the southern end of the Piute Mountains, was established to provide a military presence in the desert and to protect pioneer travelers on their westward journeys. Indians resisted the intrusion of settlers on tribal lands; there were frequent attacks on westbound settlers and mail wagons traveling the route from Prescott, Arizona, to Los Angeles.

Subsequent military escorts protected travelers, but conditions at the outpost were intolerable for many soldiers stationed at Fort Piute. Desertion was a regular occurrence, and the outpost was officially staffed by just eighteen men of the Company "D" Ninth Infantry Division from 1867 to 1868.

Today the small, primitive installation lies in ruins; its thick rock-and-mortar walls have been weathered and crumbled to a height of just 2 or 3 feet. The stone outlines of the original buildings delineate three connecting rooms that served as a tiny living quarters, corral, and cookhouse.

The walk along Piute Creek is of more than military interest. The only perennial stream in the East Mojave, Piute Creek waters an oasislike area where cottonwoods, willows, and sedges flourish. Bighorn sheep frequently visit this watering site, as do a large number of birds. (This is a fragile ecosystem, not a recreation area. Please treat the creek gently.)

The hike explores Piute Creek and gorge and gives you a chance to walk a portion of the historic Mojave Road. Following the Mojave Road Trail, as it's called, lets you walk back in time and get a glimpse of the hardships faced by early pioneers.

This is not a hike for the inexperienced or for first-time visitors to Mojave National Preserve; the roads and paths are unsigned and sometimes hard to follow.

Experienced hikers and repeat visitors, however, will thoroughly enjoy their exploration of Fort Piute.

Directions to trailhead: Head west on Interstate 40 and take the turnoff for the road leading to the hamlet of Goffs. Pass through Goffs and drive 16 miles along Lanfair Road to a point about 100 feet beyond its junction with Cedar Canyon Road. Turn right (east) on a road that goes by four names: Cedar Canyon Road, the utility road, Cable Road, and Pole Road. The last three names arise from the fact that the road follows a buried telephone cable. Drive east, staying right at a junction 3⁷⁄₁₀ miles out, and sticking with the cable road about 6 more miles to another junction where there's a cattle guard. Turn left before the cattle guard onto another dirt road and proceed a mile to a corral and the unsigned trailhead.

The walk: From the corral, head almost due south toward a gate, almost ½-mile from the start, which lets you through a fence and onto the old Mojave Road. (Remember to close the gate.)

Now you begin climbing Piute Hill. From atop the hill, catch your breath and admire the view of Table Mountain directly to the west and Castle Peaks to the north.

One look at the road gives you some idea of the hardships experienced by pioneers who passed this way 130 years ago. Piute Hill was said to be among the most feared obstacles of the westward crossing. Hikers can still see the deep ruts carved in rock by the heavy wagons.

On the way to the fort you'll pass a long, loose, sandy trail near Piute Creek, where there's nice picnicking. (The water in the creek is not safe to drink.)

About ½-mile from the fort, you'll cross the creek. On the other side, the Mojave Road narrows. Look sharply for the Piute Canyon Trail coming in from the west. (This will be your return route.) Continue on a slight descent to the fort.

An interpretive marker provides historical information about "Fort Pah Ute, 1867–68." Don't sit on the walls or disturb the ruins; like all cultural resources in the desert, the fort is protected by federal law.

Head back along the Mojave Road ½-mile, bearing right on unsigned Piute Canyon Trail. This narrow path stays high on the canyon wall, heading west at first, then north. A ½-mile along, you can see prominent Piute Gorge to the west; you'll follow this gorge back to the trailhead.

At the bottom, you'll proceed west up Piute Gorge; stay on the gorge bottom. After ½-mile you'll come to an intersection where another canyon comes in from the left. Don't take this route, but continue up the gorge to the right.

A little farther along, a trail leading out of the gorge takes off from the left (keep a sharp eye out for this one). Take this trail up to the rim of the gorge, where there's a scenic overlook. From here, follow the dirt road south back to the trailhead.

Intriguing petroglyphs abound in this part of the East Mojave.

Mid Hills and Hole-in-the-Wall

Mid Hills to Hole-in-the-Wall Trail

Terrain: Red-rock canyon, basin, and mesas.
Highlights: Diverse desert scenery viewed from best trail in the preserve.
Distance: From Mid Hills Campground to Hole-in-the-Wall Campground is 8 miles one way with 1,000-foot elevation loss.
Degree of difficulty: Moderate.

Hole-in-the-Wall and Mid Hills are the centerpieces of Mojave National Preserve. Both locales offer diverse desert scenery and fine campgrounds. Doubling the pleasure of these special places is an 8-mile trail that links them together.

Mile-high Mid Hills recalls the Great Basin desert topography of Nevada and Utah. It's 1,000 or so feet higher than Hole-in-the-Wall and thus, as a starting point, offers the hiker an easier way to go.

Mid Hills, so named because of its location halfway between the Providence and New York mountains, offers a grand observation point from which to gaze out at the East Mojave's dominant mountain ranges: the coffee with cream–colored Pinto Mountains to the north and the rolling Kelso Dunes shining on the western horizon. Looking northwest, you'll also get a superb view of Cima Dome, the 75-square-mile chunk of uplifted volcanic rock.

Hole-in-the-Wall is a second inviting locale, the kind of place Butch Cassidy and the Sundance Kid might have chosen as a hideout. Hole-in-the-Wall is a twisted maze of red rock. Geologists call this rhyolite, a kind of lava that existed as hot liquid far below the earth's surface, then crystallized.

A series of iron rings aids descent into Banshee Canyon. The rings are not particularly difficult for those who are reasonably agile and take their time.

If you're not up for a long day hike, the ¾-mile trip from Hole-in-the-Wall Campground to Banshee Canyon and the 5-mile jaunt to Wildhorse Canyon offer some easier alternatives.

A word about desert hiking in general and this desert hike in particular: You'll often travel in the bottom of sandy washes instead of over more clearly defined trails found in forest locales. This means the hiker must rely on maps, a sense of direction, rock cairns, and installed signs.

This hike is an adventurous excursion through a diverse desert environment. You'll see basin and range tabletop mesas, large pinyon pine trees, an array of colorful cacti, and lichen-covered granite rocks. East Mojave views—Table Mountain, Wildhorse Mesa, the Providence Range—are unparalleled.

Directions to trailhead: From Interstate 40, approximately 42 miles west of Needles and nearly 100 miles east of Barstow, exit on Essex Road. Head north 9½ miles to the junction of Essex Road and Black Canyon Road. Bear right on the latter road, which soon turns

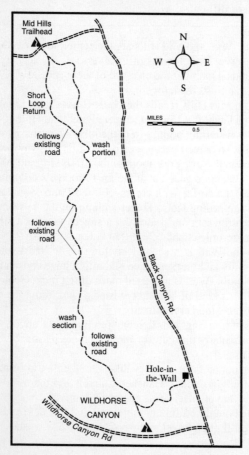

to dirt. (Well-graded Black Canyon Road is suitable for passenger cars.) After 8½ miles of travel you'll spot Hole-in-the-Wall Campground on your left. Turn into the campground and park at the lip of Banshee Canyon on the upper loop of the camp road. The unsigned trail plunges right into the canyon.

Those wishing to park vehicles for day hikes on the trail are encouraged to use the new Wildhorse Canyon Trailhead on Wildhorse Canyon Road.

Another 9 or so miles of travel on Black Canyon Road brings you to the signed turnoff for Mid Hills Campground. You'll turn left and drive 2 miles to the campground. The Mid Hills trailhead is located next to a windmill immediately opposite the entrance road to the campground.

The walk: In a short distance, the path ascends to a saddle that offers splendid views of the Pinto Valley to the northeast. (The saddle is this hike's high point.)

From the saddle, the path angles south, descending into, then climbing out of a wash. Keep a close eye on the trail; it's easy to lose here.

The trail reaches a dirt road, follows it for a mere 100 feet, then turns sharply left to join a wash for a time, leaves it, and crosses a road. You encounter another wash, enter it, and exit it.

After a modest ascent, the trail joins a road, passes through a gate, and joins another road for a little more than a mile. This road serves up spectacular views to the south of the Providence Mountains and Wildhorse Mesa.

Next to a group of large boulders, a road veers left but hikers bear right, soon turning sharp left with the road. The route passes through another gate, then works its way through a dense thicket of cholla cactus.

After following another wash, the trail crosses a dirt road, then soon joins a second road, which follows a wash to a dead end at an abandoned dam. The trail ascends through some rocks, levels for a time, then descends. A ¼-mile before trail's end, you'll spy the Hole-in-the-Wall spur trail leading off to the left.

Kelso Dunes

Kelso Dunes Trail

Terrain: One of tallest dune complexes in America.
Highlights: "Booming" dunes, grand views.
Distance: To top of Kelso Dunes is 3 miles round-trip with 400-foot elevation gain.
Degree of difficulty: Easy to moderate.

In the heart of the East Mojave lie the Kelso Dunes, one of the tallest dune systems in America. And the dunes give off good vibrations, say many desert day hikers.

The good vibrations that enthuse hikers are not the desert's spiritual emanations—which many visitors find considerable—but the Kelso Dunes' rare ability to make a low rumbling sound when sand slides down their steep slopes. This sound has been variously compared with that of a kettledrum, a low-flying airplane, and a Tibetan gong.

The sand that forms Kelso Dunes blows in from the Mojave River basin. After traveling east 35 miles across a stark plain known as the Devil's Playground, it's deposited in hills nearly 600 feet high. The westerlies carrying the sand rush headlong into winds from other directions, which is why the sand is dropped here, and why it stays here.

For further confirmation of the circular pattern of winds that formed the dunes, examine the bunches of grass on the lower slopes. You'll notice that the tips of the tall grasses have etched complete circles on the sand.

Other patterns on the sand are made by the desert's abundant, but rarely seen, wildlife. You might see the tracks of a coyote, kit fox, antelope ground squirrel, pack rat, raven, or sidewinder. Footprints of lizards and mice can be seen tacking this way and that over the sand. The dune's surface records the lightest pressure of the smallest feet.

Directions to trailhead: From Interstate 15 in Baker, 60 miles northeast of Barstow, turn south on Kelbaker Road and proceed about 35 miles to the town of Kelso. Pause to admire the classic neo-Spanish-style Kelso Railroad Depot next to the Union Pacific tracks. The building is being restored as a visitor center.

From Kelso, continue on Kelbaker Road for another 7 miles to a signed dirt road and turn right (west). Drive slowly along this road (navigable for all but very low-slung passenger cars) 3 miles to a parking area. The trail to Kelso Dunes begins just up the dirt road from the parking area.

The walk: Only the first ¼-mile or so of the walk to the dunes is on established trail. Once the trail peters out, angle toward the low saddle atop the dunes, just to the right of the highest point.

You've heard the old saying "One step forward, two steps back"? This saying will take on new meaning if you attempt to take the most direct route to the top of the dunes by walking straight up the tallest sand hill.

As you cross the lower dunes, you'll pass some mesquite and cre-osote bushes. During spring of a good wildflower year, the lower dunes are bedecked with yellow and white desert primrose, pink sand verbena, and yellow sunflowers.

When you reach the saddle located to the right of the high point, turn left and trek another 100 yards or so to the top. The black ma-terial crowning the top of the dunes is magnetite, an iron oxide, and one of about two dozen minerals found within the dune system.

Enjoy the view from the top: the Kelso Mountains to the north, the Bristol Mountains to the southwest, the Granite Mountains to the south, the Providence Mountains to the east. Everywhere you look there are mountain ranges, small and large. In fact, despite

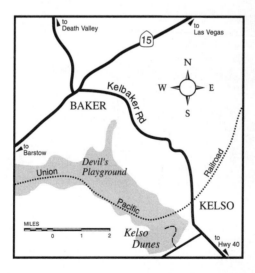

evidence to the contrary—most notably the stunning dunes beneath your feet—the East Mojave is really a desert of mountains, not sand.

While atop the dunes, perhaps your footsteps will cause mini-avalanches and the dunes will sha-boom-sha-boom for you. There's speculation that the extreme dryness of the East Mojave, combined with the rounded, wind-polished shape of the sand grains, has something to do with their musical ability. After picking up good vibrations, descend the steep dune face (much easier on the way down!) and return to the trailhead.

Kelso Dunes—the perfect place for quiet contemplation.

⚤ Mitchell Caverns

Mitchell Caverns Trail

> **Terrain:** Limestone cave.
> **Highlights:** Guided hike of the caverns.
> **Distance:** 1½ miles round-trip.
> **Degree of difficulty:** Easy.

Trail trivia question: Where in California can you explore some stunning scenery, be assured that it won't rain, and know that the temperature for your hike will always be a comfortable 65°F?

Hint: One of the overlooked gems of the California state park system.

If you're in the dark, then you're on the right path—the trail through Mitchell Caverns State Reserve, part of Providence Mountains State Recreation Area. Ranger-led walks through the dramatic limestone caves offer a fascinating geology lesson, one the whole family can enjoy.

In 1932 Jack Mitchell abandoned his Depression-shattered business in Los Angeles and moved to the desert. For a time he prospected for silver, but his real fascination was with what he called the Providence or Crystal caves and their potential as a tourist attraction. He constructed several stone buildings to use for lodging. (Today's park visitor center is one of these buildings.) Mitchell and his wife, Ida, provided food, lodging, and guided tours of the caverns until 1954. By all accounts, Jack Mitchell was quite a yarn-spinner. Old-timers still remember his tall tales of ghosts, lost treasure, and bottomless pits.

Now that the caverns are part of the state park system, rangers lead the tours. They're an enthusiastic lot and quite informative. Visitors walk through the two main caves, which Mitchell named El Pakiva (The Devil's House) and Tecopa (after a Shoshonean chieftain). You'll get a close-up view of stalactites and stalagmites, cave ribbon, cave spaghetti, and flow stone. And you'll learn about some of the caverns' former inhabitants—the Chemehuevi Indians and a Pleistocene ground sloth that stumbled into the darkness some 15,000 years ago.

In Jack Mitchell's day, visitors had to be nimble rock-climbers who waited for their tour leader to toss flares into the darkness. Nowadays, the caverns are equipped with stairs and special lighting.

Guided tours are conducted Monday through Friday at 1:30 P.M. On Saturday and Sunday, tours begin at 10:00 A.M., 1:30 P.M., and 3:00 P.M. A fee is charged. The tour takes between 1½ and 2 hours, depending on your group's enthusiasm and collective curiosity.

Directions to trailhead: From Interstate 40, about 80 miles east of Barstow, exit on Essex Road and drive 16 miles to road's end at the Providence Mountains State Recreation Area parking lot. Sign up at the visitor center for tours.

The walk: Because you can tour the caverns only with a park ranger, and because you wouldn't want me to spoil the many surprises of the cave walk with a step-by-step description, I won't further detail the Mitchell Caverns Trail. However, after exploring "the great indoors," allow some time to investigate the park's outdoor pathways.

Pick up an interpretive booklet from the park visitor center and walk the ½-mile Mary Beal Nature Trail, which offers a great introduction to high desert flora. Cliffrose and blue sage share the hillsides with cholla, catclaw, and creosote.

The trail honors Mary Beal, a Riverside librarian who at the turn of the century was "exiled" to the desert by her doctor for health reasons. For a half-century this remarkable woman wandered through the Providence Mountains and other remote Mojave Desert locales gathering and classifying hundreds of varieties of wildflowers and other plants. The trail was dedicated in 1952 on Beal's seventy-fifth birthday.

The short Overlook Trail leads from the park's tiny campground to a viewpoint, which offers vistas of Clipper Valley, the Marble Mountains, and hundreds of square miles of basin and range topography.

The 1-mile Crystal Spring Trail leads into the pinyon pine– and juniper-dotted Providence Mountains by way of Crystal Canyon. Bighorn sheep often travel through this canyon.

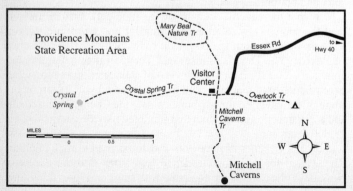

4. Joshua Tree National Park

For many visitors, the Joshua trees are not only the essence but the whole of their experience at Joshua Tree National Park. The park, however, is much more than a tableau of twisted yucca. It beckons the explorer with a diversity of desert environments, including sand dunes, native palm oases, cactus gardens, and jumbles of jumbo granite.

The Joshua tree's distribution defines the very boundaries of the Mojave Desert. Here in its namesake national park it reaches the southernmost limit of its range.

The park area is sometimes known as the "connecting" desert because of its location between the Mojave and the Colorado deserts, and because it shares characteristics of each. The Mojave, a desert of mountains, is (relatively) cooler, wetter, and higher; it forms the northern and western parts of the park. Southern and eastern sections of the park are part of the hotter, drier, lower Colorado Desert, characterized by a wide variety of desert flora, including ironwood, smoke tree, and native California fan palms. Cacti, especially cholla and ocotillo, thrive in the more southerly Colorado Desert (a part of the larger Sonoran Desert).

In 1994, under provisions of the federal California Desert Protection Act, Joshua Tree was "upgraded" to national park status and expanded by about a quarter-million acres. The park attracts campers, hikers, and especially rock climbers. From Hidden Valley to the Wonderland of Rocks, the park has emerged as one of the world's premier rock-climbing destinations. The park offers about 3,000 climbing routes, ranging from the easiest of bouldering to some of the sport's most difficult technical climbs.

The visitor center is located alongside one of the park's four palm oases—the Oasis of Mara, also know as Twentynine Palms. For many hundreds of years Native Americans lived at "the place of little springs and much grass."

Two paved roads explore the heart of the park. The first loops through the high northwest section, visiting Queen and Lost Horse valleys, as well as the awesome boulder piles at Jumbo Rocks and Wonderland of Rocks. The second angles northwest–southeast across the park; it crosses both the Mojave Desert's Joshua tree woodland and the Colorado Desert's cactus gardens.

From Oasis Visitor Center, drive south to Jumbo Rocks, which is kind of Joshua Tree National Park to the max: a vast array of rock formations, a Joshua tree forest, the yucca-dotted desert open and wide. Check out Skull Rock—one of the many rocks in the area that appear to resemble human beings, dinosaurs, monsters, cathedrals, and castles—by taking a nature trail (1½ miles) that provides an introduction to the park's flora, wildlife, and geology.

In Queen Valley, just west of Jumbo Rocks, is the signed beginning of Geology Tour Road, a rough dirt road (four-wheel drive recommended) extending 18 miles into the heart of the park. Motorists get close-up looks at the considerable erosive forces that shaped this land, forming the flattest of desert playas, or dry lake beds, as well as massive heaps of boulders that tower over the valley floor. Some good hikes begin off Geology Tour Road, which delivers a Joshua tree woodland, a historic spring, abandoned mines, and some fascinating native petroglyphs.

Farther west is Indian Cave, typical of the kind of shelter sought by the nomadic Cahuilla and Serrano Indian clans that traveled this desert land. A number of bedrock mortars found in the cave suggest its use as a work site by its aboriginal inhabitants. A 4-mile round-trip trail climbs through a lunar landscape of rocks and Joshua trees to the top of 5,470-foot Ryan Mountain. Your reward for the climb is one of the park's best views.

At Cap Rock Junction, the paved park road swings north toward the Wonderland of Rocks, 12 square miles of massive jumbled granite. This curious maze of stone hides groves of Joshua trees, trackless washes, and several small pools of water.

The easiest and certainly the safest way to explore the Wonderland is to follow the Barker Dam Loop Trail (1¼ miles). The first part of the journey is on a nature trail that interprets botanical highlights; the second part visits some native petroglyphs and a little lake created a century ago by cattle ranchers.

Cottonwood Spring, near the south end of the park, is a little palm- and cottonwood-shaded oasis that attracts desert birds and bird-watchers. From Cottonwood Campground a trail leads to the old Mastodon Gold Mine, then climbs behemoth-looking Mastodon Peak for a view from Mount San Jacinto above Palm Springs to the Salton Sea.

The national park holds two more of California's loveliest palm oases. Fortynine Palms Oasis Trail winds up and over a hot rocky crest to the dripping springs, to pools and the blessed shade of palms and cottonwoods. Lost Palms Oasis Trail visits the park's premier palm grove.

You'll see plenty of Joshua trees along the park's pathways, but there's much more for the hiker to discover. One of my favorite footpaths is Black Rock Canyon Trail, which follows a classic desert wash, then ascends to the crest of the Little San Bernardino Mountains at Warren Peak. Desert and mountain views from the peak are stunning. Another favorite is Lost Horse Mine Trail; it visits one of the area's most successful gold mines, offering a look back into a colorful era and some fine views into the heart of the park.

The upturned limbs of the Joshua tree are dramatically silhouetted at day's end.

Black Rock Canyon

Black Rock Canyon Trail

> **Terrain:** High-desert canyon, juniper- and pinyon pine–dotted crest of Little San Bernardino Mountains.
> **Highlights:** Joshua trees, desert flora–filled wash, panoramic views.
> **Distance:** From Black Rock Canyon Campground to Warren Peak is 6 miles round-trip with 1,000-foot elevation gain.
> **Degree of difficulty:** Moderate to strenuous.

A hike through Black Rock Canyon has just about everything a desert hike should have: plenty of cactus, pinyon pine–dotted peaks, a sandy wash, dramatic rock formations, a hidden spring, grand vistas. And much more.

Tucked away in the northwest corner of the park, the Black Rock Canyon area also hosts forests of the shaggy Joshuas. *Yucca brevifolia* thrive at the higher elevations of this end of the national park.

More than 200 species of birds, including speedy roadrunners, have been observed in and around Black Rock Canyon. Hikers frequently spot mule deer and rabbits—desert cottontails and black-tailed jackrabbits. Bighorn sheep are also sighted occasionally.

A bit off the tourist track, Black Rock Canyon rarely makes the must-see list of natural attractions at the national park; the park brochure contains no mention of the canyon. Ironically, though, while Black Rock is often overlooked, it is one of the easiest places to reach. The canyon is close to Yucca Valley's commercial strip, very close to a residential neighborhood.

Maybe we nature lovers practice a curious logic: If a beautiful place is near civilization it can't be that beautiful, right? In Black Rock Canyon's case, our logic would be faulty. The canyon matches the allure of much more remote regions of the national park.

Black Rock Canyon's proximity to civilization might even work to the advantage of the rough-it deluxe crowd. Happy campers in the canyon's fine campground can take the 5-mile drive into Yucca Valley for dinner. (No one gets K.P.) You can travel from town to the trailhead in a few minutes.

Black Rock Canyon Trail follows a classic desert wash, then ascends to the crest of the Little San Bernardino Mountains at Warren Peak. Desert and mountain views from the peak are stunning.

Directions to trailhead: From Highway 62 (Twentynine Palms Highway) in Yucca Valley, turn south on Joshua Lane and drive 5 miles through a residential area to Black Rock Ranger Station. Park at the station, which has some interpretive displays and sells books and maps. Ask rangers for the latest trail information.

Walk uphill through the campground to campsite 30 and the trailhead.

The walk: From the upper end of the campground, the trail leads to a water tank, goes left a very short distance on a park service road, then angles right. After a few hundred yards, the trail splits. The main trail descends directly into Black Rock Canyon wash. (An upper trail crests a hill before it, too, descends into the wash.)

A ¼-mile from the trailhead, the path drops into the dry, sandy creek bed of Black Rock Canyon. You'll bear right and head up the wide canyon mouth, passing Joshua trees, desert willow, and cholla.

A mile of wash-walking leads you to the remains of some so-called tanks—rock basins built by early ranchers to hold water for their cattle.

Another ¼-mile up the wash is Black Rock Spring, sometimes dry, sometimes a trickle. Beyond the spring, the canyon narrows. You wend your way around beavertail cactus, pinyon pine, and juniper.

Near the head of the canyon, the trail splits. (Turning left [east] cross-country would lead you along a rough ridge to Peak 5195.) If you follow the right fork of the rough trail, you'll climb to a dramatic ridge crest of the Little San Bernardino Mountains, then angle

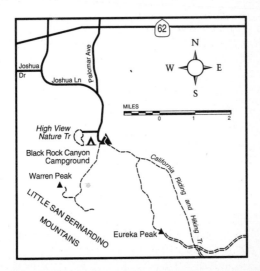

right (west) along the crest. A steep, ¼-mile ascent past contorted, windblown juniper and pinyon pine brings you to the top of Warren Peak.

Oh, what a grand clear-day view! North is the Mojave Desert. To the west is snowy Mount San Gorgonio, Southern California's highest peak, as well as the San Bernardino Mountains and the deep trough of San Gorgonio Pass. Southwest lies mighty Mount San Jacinto, and to the south (this is often the murky part of the view), Palm Springs and the Coachella Valley. The peaks of the Little San Bernardino Mountains extend southeast, marching toward the Salton Sea.

Eureka Peak

California Riding and Hiking Trail,
Eureka Peak Trail

Terrain: Wash, canyon, steep slopes.
Highlights: One of best views in the park.
Distance: From Black Rock Canyon Campground to Eureka
   Peak is 11 miles round-trip with 1,500-foot elevation gain.
Degree of difficulty: Strenuous.

Many hikers claim the panoramic view from 5,516-foot Eureka Peak is one of the best in the national park. In winter and spring, snowcapped Mount San Jacinto towers over the Coachella Valley. Mount San Gorgonio, the highest peak in Southern California, and other 10,000-foot summits in the San Gorgonio Wilderness are also a majestic sight.

Hikers may lament the fact that motorists can drive to within 100 yards of Eureka Peak and get the same view. Nevertheless, using two feet instead of four wheels to climb Eureka has much to recommend it.

From Black Rock Campground, a 2-mile length of the California Riding and Hiking Trail ascends the hills fringing the Yucca Valley, then delivers you to a series of washes and narrow canyons that you follow to the summit of Eureka Peak. Orange-blazed posts help you negotiate the trailless stretches of the route.

Once atop the peak, you have several options: returning to Black Rock Campground on the same trail; having a friend pick you up at the peak (my favorite option); or continuing 2 miles by dirt road to Covington Flat and then getting a ride. The only option I'd advise against is taking the California Riding and Hiking Trail from Black Rock to the peak, then taking the cross-country route down from Eureka Peak; the latter route is very difficult to negotiate and to navigate going downhill from south to north.

Directions to trailhead: From Highway 62 (Twentynine Palms Highway) in Yucca Valley, turn south on Joshua Lane and drive 5 miles through a residential area to Black Rock Ranger Station. Park at the station. Signed California Riding and Hiking Trail is located on the east side of Black Rock Campground.

101

The walk: The trail passes through some pretty country dotted with Joshua trees, pinyon pine, and juniper. Enjoy the view of the fast-developing Yucca Valley. After 2 miles, the path reaches a convergence of two washes. The California Riding and Hiking Trail heads east, but your route is the south fork to the right.

After ½-mile or so, the wash forks and you'll bear right, following this branch of the wash 2 miles to its end, then heading left (southeast) over a ridge. Cresting this ridge, you'll continue to angle south-southeast around to the south side of Eureka Peak. Lastly, you'll join the short summit trail (and those motorists taking the easy way to the top!) ascending from the parking area.

Savor the view. Then, if you're hiking the loop, descend the dirt road 1 mile to its intersection with the California Riding and Hiking Trail on the left (north) side of the road. It's mostly mellow walking and a moderate descent 3 miles to where the trail junctions with the wash you followed up to Eureka Peak. Two more miles of walking on the riding and hiking trail past Joshua trees brings you back to the trailhead.

Rattlesnake Canyon

Rattlesnake Canyon Cross-country Route

Terrain: Intriguing slot canyon, polished rocks.
Highlights: Seasonal pools, cascades, waterfall.
Distance: 1 to 6 miles round-trip.
Degree of difficulty: Moderate to strenuous.

The northern access point to the famed 10-square-mile Wonderland of Rocks is Indian Cove. This favorite camping spot and picnic area is the jumping-off spot for an exploration of one of the Wonderland's more intriguing slot canyons—Rattlesnake Canyon.

Considering this is known as one of the drier areas of the park, it's surprising to discover a (seasonal) little creek flowing through boulder-strewn Rattlesnake Canyon. A ½-mile from the mouth of the canyon is a small waterfall, where the creek tumbles over the polished rocks. Tiny cascades and some lovely pools complete the attractive scene.

Not only is Rattlesnake Canyon easy on the eye, it's pleasing to the ear when water is flowing. The reverberation of the running water in the narrow canyon overwhelms all sounds of nearby civilization. At night, the soprano peeping of the resident tree frogs echoes through the canyon.

Beyond the waterfall area, Rattlesnake Canyon is difficult to traverse and recommended only for experienced hikers with boulder-scrambling experience.

Directions to trailhead: From Yucca Valley, drive east on Highway 62 for 14 miles to Indian Cove Road. Turn south (right), proceed a mile to the ranger station, then another 3³⁄₁₀ miles to the picnic area at road's end.

The walk: From the picnic area, march east into what is usually the dry creek bed of Rattlesnake Canyon. Head south (up-canyon), dodging creosote bushes and yucca and working your way around the canyon's many boulders to the base of the falls.

Experienced hikers will climb around and above the falls and continue up-canyon. After much scrambling, you'll eventually reach a sandy wash and a more open part of the canyon.

Fortynine Palms

Fortynine Palms Trail

> **Terrain:** Palm-filled canyon.
> **Highlights:** Tranquil, accessible oasis.
> **Distance:** To Fortynine Palms Oasis is 3 miles round-trip with 400-foot elevation gain.
> **Degree of difficulty:** Easy to moderate.

Fortynine Palms Oasis, reached only by trail, has retained a wonderful air of remoteness. From the parking area, an old Indian trail climbs a steep ridge and offers the hiker expansive views of the Sheephole and Bullion mountain ranges.

On the exposed ridge, barrel cacti, creosote, yucca, and brittlebush brave the heat. As the trail winds up and over a rocky crest, the restful green of the oasis comes into view.

At the oasis, nature's personality abruptly changes and the dry, sunbaked ridges give way to dripping springs, pools, and the blessed shade of palms and cottonwoods.

Unlike some oases, which are strung out for miles along a stream, Fortynine Palms is a close-knit palm family centered around a generous supply of surface water. Seeps and springs fill numerous basins set among the rocks at different levels. Other basins are supplied by "rain" drip-drip-dripping from the upper levels. Mesquite and willow thrive alongside the palms. Singing house finches and croaking frogs provide a musical interlude.

Perched on a steep canyon wall, Fortynine Palms Oasis overlooks the town of Twentynine Palms, but its untouched beauty makes it seem a lot farther removed from civilization.

Directions to trailhead: From Interstate 10, a few miles east of the Highway 111 turnoff to Palm Springs, bear north on Highway 62. After passing the town of Yucca Valley, but before reaching the outskirts of Twentynine Palms, turn right on Canyon Road. (Hint: Look for an animal hospital at the corner of Highway 62 and Canyon Road.) Follow Canyon Road 1¼ miles to its end at a National Park Service parking area and the trailhead.

The walk: The trail rises through a spartan rockscape dotted with cacti and jojoba. After a brisk climb, catch your breath atop a ridge and enjoy the view of Twentynine Palms and the surrounding desert.

You may notice colorful patches of lichen adhering to the rocks. Lichen, which conducts the business of life as a limited partnership of algae and fungi, is very sensitive to air pollution; the health of this tiny plant is considered by some botanists to be a gauge of air quality. Contemplate the abstract impressionist patterns of the lichen, inhale great draughts of fresh air, then follow the trail as it descends from the ridge top.

The trail leads down slopes dotted with barrel cactus and mesquite. Soon the oasis comes into view. Lucky hikers may get a fleeting glimpse of bighorn sheep drinking from oasis pools or gamboling over nearby steep slopes.

As the path leads you to the palms, you'll notice many fire-blackened tree trunks. The grove has burned several times since this land was set aside a half-century ago and placed under the protection of the National Park Service.

Fortunately, palms are among the most fireproof trees in existence, and fire—whether caused by human beings or lightning—seldom kills them. Fire may actually benefit the palms because it temporarily eliminates competition from trees such as mesquite and cottonwood and from bushes like arrowweed, all of them thirsty fellows and able to push their roots much deeper in search of water than palms. Burning also opens the oasis floor to sunlight, which seedling palms need.

Fortynine Palms Oasis celebrates life. Native California fan palms cluster near handsome boulder-lined pools. Fuzzy cattails, ferns, and

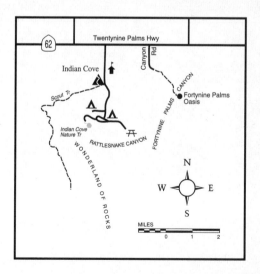

grasses sway in the breeze. An oasis like this one gives the hiker a chance to view the desert in terms that are the exact opposite of its stereotypical dry hostility. If the desert is the land God forgot, then the Creator must have had a sudden afterthought and decided to sprinkle this parched land with oases, reminders of his lush handiwork.

This palm oasis seems Heaven-sent to the weary desert hiker.

Joshua Tree National Park
Eight Nature Trails

Terrain: Jumbles of rocks, Joshua tree forests, hidden valleys.
Highlights: Easily accessible, well-interpreted wonders of national park.
Distance: ¼-mile to 1¾ miles round-trip.
Degree of difficulty: Easy.

Interpreted nature trails, ranging from ¼-mile to 1¾ miles in length, explore some of the highlights of the national park. They travel over gentle terrain and offer an ideal introduction to the wonders of the desert. My eight great nature trail picks are:

Oasis of Mara (½-mile loop)

Begin: Oasis Visitor Center.

A paved nature trail leads under rustling palms to the famed Twentynine Palms Oasis, perhaps California's most famous (and certainly the most accessible) palm oasis. To the native Serrano, *mara* meant "the place of small springs and much grass." Cattle ranchers, gold seekers, health seekers, and generations of desert lovers have found beauty and tranquillity here. A pamphlet interprets the natural history of the area.

Skull Rock (1¾-mile loop)

Begin: Jumbo Rocks Campground, beyond Loop E entrance.

This path is a sort of desert sampler—a tour through a Joshua tree forest, then over a sandscape dotted with Mojave yucca, paper-bag bushes, and many more unusual desert plants. Skull Rock and the other weathered quartz monzonite rocks in these parts have been sculpted by erosion into some fantastic shapes. (See Skull Rock walk.)

Barker Dam (1¼-mile loop)

Begin: Barker Dam Parking Area.

One of the many wonders of the park is the Wonderland of Rocks, 12 square miles of massive jumbled granite. This curious maze of stone hides groves of Joshua trees, trackless washes, and a small pool of water. The easiest and safest way to explore the Wonderland is by walking the Barker Dam Loop Trail. The path's first part interprets the botanical highlights of the area; the second part visits some Native American petroglyphs.

Hidden Valley (1-mile loop)

Begin: Hidden Valley Picnic Area.

A moonscape of buttes and towers, this strange valley is entered by a narrow gap in the rock walls. Legend has it that cattle rustlers and horse thieves used the remote, rock-rimmed valley as a hideout. Signs along the nature trail tell the story of the vegetation that manages to survive in this rugged and rocky habitat.

Cap Rock (⅖-mile loop)

Begin: Cap Rock Parking Area.

Perched atop a monolithic dome is a visor-shaped boulder resembling the bill on a baseball cap. Signs along the nature trail interpret Mojave Desert geology and plant life. The level, paved path is wheelchair accessible.

Keys View (¼-mile loop)

Begin: Keys View.

Not much of a trail, but oh, what a view! A paved pathway leads to a commanding viewpoint where visitors can observe several points of interest: Mount San Gorgonio, Mount San Jacinto above Palm Springs, the Salton Sea, and the San Andreas Fault.

Cholla Cactus Garden (¼-mile loop)

Begin: Pinto Basin Road near mile 10.

An easy path, accompanied by an interpretive pamphlet, introduces visitors to desert flora. The highlight of this walk is a dense concentration of Bigelow cholla, often called "teddy bear" cactus because of the (deceptively) soft, even fluffy appearance of its sharp spines. (Don't touch or you'll be sorry!)

Cottonwood (1 mile)

Begin: Cottonwood Campground sites 13A and 13B.

An interpreted nature trail travels through rolling hills on its way to Cottonwood Spring Oasis, haven for birds and desert wildlife. Nearby are some Native American bedrock mortars.

Hidden in the Wonderland of Rocks—Barker Dam.

Desert Queen Mine

Desert Queen Mine Trail

Terrain: Pinyon pine– and juniper-dotted wash.
Highlights: Ruins of fabled mine.
Distance: 1⅓ miles round-trip.
Degree of difficulty: Easy.

Perched atop cliffs north of Jumbo Rocks Campground are the considerable ruins of the Desert Queen Mine, one of the more profitable gold mines dug in the desert now called Joshua Tree National Park. Shafts, stone building foundations, and rusting machinery are scattered about the slopes above Desert Queen Wash.

If murder and intrigue are what fascinate us about desert mines, then the Desert Queen is quite a story. The tale begins in 1894 when a prospector named Frank James discovered some rich gold ore in the hills north of Jumbo Rocks. Word of his discovery reached cattle rustler Jim McHaney, who, as the story goes, ordered his men to follow James to his claim and talk things over. One of McHaney's thugs, Charles Martin, shot James dead (though an inquest jury decided that Martin had acted in self-defense and did not need to stand trial). Jim McHaney and his more respectable brother Bill owned the Desert Queen for two years; however, the $30,000 to $40,000 yielded by a good-sized pocket of ore was squandered by high-living Jim (later to be convicted of counterfeiting), and the bank reclaimed the mine.

Hard-rock miner William Keys took control of the mine in 1915; Altadena jeweler Frederick Morton, in 1931. Morton was convinced by a dubious "mining engineer" to acquire and to invest heavily in the Desert Queen. Against all odds, the miners under the supervision of "Mr. Hapwell" actually struck pay dirt. Hapwell set up a secret stamp mill nearby to process the ore and, of course, pocketed the profits. Meanwhile the fast-going-broke Morton sold stock in the Desert Queen without incorporating—a violation of securities law that soon got him convicted of fraud. The mysterious (and by some accounts wealthy) Mr. Hapwell dropped out of sight.

You can visit the ruins of the Desert Queen from a northern trailhead shared with the path to Pine City or from a southern trailhead at Split Rock Picnic Area.

Directions to trailhead: From the park highway, opposite Geology Tour Road, turn right (north) and drive 1¼ miles to a parking area for the mine.

The walk: The path, an old mine road, heads east past some building foundations. The trail forks. The right fork splits south and travels 2 miles, past the site of the Eagle Cliff Mine to Split Rock Picnic Area.

Adventurous walkers can take the left fork, climb a bit through pinyon pine– and juniper-dotted Desert Queen Wash, pass a mining area called John's Camp, and travel 3 miles to the park road.

Ivanpah Tanks

Ivanpah Tanks Trail

> **Terrain:** Desert wash.
> **Highlights:** Historic "tanks."
> **Distance:** 1-mile loop.
> **Degree of difficulty:** Easy.

Ivanpah is one of the many tanks—rock- and cement-lined water catchment basins—built by turn-of-the-century cattle ranchers. (See Barker Dam walk.) This walk visits Ivanpah Tank and Live Oak Tank, both holding more sand than water these days, by way of a handsome little desert wash.

Live Oak, which names a tank, a road, and a picnic area, refers to an unusual oak that botanists believe is a hybrid of the valley oak, found between the Santa Monica Mountains near Los Angeles and the San Joaquin Valley, and the small-sized turbinella oak, which thrives in the park's uplands.

Ivanpah Tanks Trail follows a wash past the famed oak to Live Oak and Ivanpah tanks, then loops back to the picnic area.

Directions to trailhead: The path begins at the west end of Live Oak Picnic Area.

The walk: From the picnic area, head south toward the big old oak located at the base of the rock cluster known as the Pope's Hat. Down-canyon a short distance from the "Live Oak" is a low stone wall—what remains of Live Oak Tank.

The sandy wash angles east below rocky, juniper-studded canyon walls, soon opening up a bit and reaching sand-filled Ivanpah Tank.

Energetic hikers may continue following the wash down-canyon a mile or so. Otherwise, ascend the left wall of the wash and return by a dirt road that once provided access to Ivanpah Tank. The old road leads to the east side of the picnic area, whereupon you follow the picnic ground road back to the trailhead.

Wonderland of Rocks

Barker Dam Loop Trail

Terrain: Jumble of granite rocks.
Highlights: Nature trail, historic Barker Dam.
Distance: Through Wonderland of Rocks to Barker Dam
is 1¼ miles round-trip.
Degree of difficulty: Easy.

One of the many wonders of Joshua Tree National Monument is the Wonderland of Rocks, 12 square miles of massive jumbled granite. This curious maze of stone hides groves of Joshua trees, trackless washes, and several small pools of water.

Perhaps the easiest and certainly the safest way to explore the Wonderland is to follow the Barker Dam Loop Trail. The first part of the journey is on a nature trail that interprets the botanical highlights of the area. The last part of the loop trail visits some Native American petroglyphs.

This hike's main destination is the small lake created by Barker Dam. A century ago, cowboys took advantage of the water catchment of this natural basin and brought their cattle to this corner of the Wonderland of Rocks. Barker and Shay Cattle Company constructed the dam, which was later raised to its present height by Bill Keys and his family in the 1950s. Family members inscribed their names atop the dam's south wall and renamed it Bighorn Dam; however, Barker was the name that stuck.

The trail to Barker Dam, while interesting, is not likely to occupy the intrepid day hiker for long. One way to explore a little more of the Wonderland of Rocks is to pick up the Wonderland Wash Ranch Trail to the Astrodomes. Departing from the next spur road and parking area past the Barker Dam trailhead, this path leads to the ruins of the pink Worth Bagley House. From the back corner of the house, you'll pick up a wash and follow an intermittent trail through boulder clusters. This trail is popular with rock climbers, who use it to reach the Astrodomes—steep, 300-foot-tall rocks that tower above the wash.

A myriad of narrow canyons and washes lead into the Wonderland, but route-finding is extremely complex and recommended only for very experienced map-and-compass users.

By park service regulation, the area is open only from 8:00 A.M. to 6:00 P.M.; this restriction is designed to allow the shy bighorn sheep a chance to reach water without human interference.

Directions to trailhead: From I–10, a little east of the Highway 111 turnoff to Palm Springs, take Highway 62 northeast to the town of Joshua Tree. Continue 4 miles south to the park entrance, then another 10 miles to Hidden Valley Campground. A dirt road leads 2 miles from Hidden Valley Campground to Barker Dam parking area.

The walk: From the north end of the parking area, join the signed trail that immediately penetrates the Wonderland of Rocks. You'll pass a special kind of oak, the turbinella, that has adjusted to the harsh conditions of desert life. The oaks are habitat for a multitude of birds and ground squirrels.

For the first ½-mile, interpretive signs point out the unique botany of this desert land. The path then squeezes through a narrow rock passageway and leads directly to the edge of the lake. Bird-watching is excellent here because many migratory species not normally associated with the desert are attracted to the lake. The morning and late afternoon hours are particularly tranquil times to visit the lake, and to contemplate the ever-changing reflections of the Wonderland of Rocks on the water.

The trail is a bit indistinct near Barker Dam but resumes again in fine form near a strange-looking circular water trough, a holdover from the area's cattle ranching days. A toiletlike float mechanism controlled the flow of water to the thirsty livestock.

The path turns south and soon passes a huge boulder known as Piano Rock. When this land was privately owned, a piano was hauled atop the rock and played for the amusement of visitors and locals.

Beyond Piano Rock the trail enters a rock-rimmed valley. A brief leftward detour at a junction brings you to the Movie Petroglyphs, so named because in less-enlightened times the native rock art was painted over by a film crew to make it more visible to the camera's eye.

Back on the main trail, you'll parallel some cliffs, perhaps get a glimpse of Indian bedrock mortars, and loop back to the parking area.

Ryan Mountain

Ryan Mountain Trail

Terrain: Rocky, mile-high peak.
Highlights: Fine summit view.
Distance: From Sheep Pass to Ryan Mountain is 4 miles round-trip with 700-foot elevation gain.
Degree of difficulty: Moderate.

This walk tours some Joshua trees, visits Indian Cave, and ascends Ryan Mountain for a nice view of the rocky wonderland in this part of Joshua Tree National Park. Ryan Mountain is named for the Ryan brothers, Thomas and Jep, who had a homestead at the base of the mountain.

Savor the view from atop Ryan Mountain. It's one of the finest in the national park.

Directions to trailhead: From the Joshua Tree National Park Visitor Center at Twentynine Palms, drive 3 miles south on Utah Trail Road (the main park road), keeping right at the Pinto Y-junction and continuing another 8 miles to Sheep Pass Campground on your left. Park in the Ryan Mountain parking area. You may also begin this hike from the Indian Cave turnout just up the road. Be sure to visit Indian Cave; a number of bedrock mortars found in the cave suggest its use as a work site by its aboriginal inhabitants.

The walk: From Sheep Pass Campground, the trail skirts the base of Ryan Mountain and passes through a lunar landscape of rocks and Joshua trees.

Soon you intersect a well-worn side trail coming up from the right. If you like, follow this brief trail down to Indian Cave, typical of the kind of shelter sought by the nomadic Cahuilla and Serrano Indian clans who once traveled this land.

Continuing past the junction, Ryan Mountain Trail ascends moderately to steeply toward the peak. En route, you'll pass some very old rocks that make up the core of this mountain and the nearby Little San Bernardino range. For eons, since their creation, these rocks have been metamorphosed by heat and pressure into completely new types, primarily gneiss and schist. No one knows their exact age, but geologists believe they're several hundred million years old.

Atop Ryan Mountain (5,470 feet) you can sign the summit register, located in a tin can stuck in a pile of rocks that marks the top of the mountain. From the peak, you're treated to a panoramic view of Lost Horse, Queen, Hidden, and Pleasant valleys. There's a lot of geologic history in the rocks shimmering on the ocean of sand below. Not all the rocks you see are as ancient as the ones on Ryan Mountain. Middle-aged rocks, predominately quartz monzonite, are found at Hidden Valley, Jumbo Rocks, and White Tank. Younger rocks made of basaltic lava are mere infants at less than a million years old; they are found in Pleasant Valley.

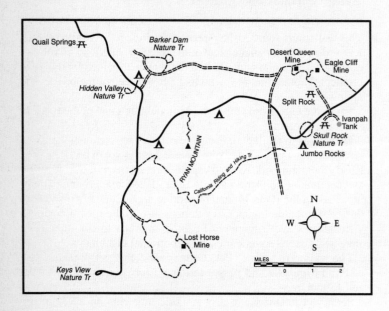

Skull Rock

Skull Rock Interpretive Trail

> **Terrain:** Jumbo Rocks, desert wash.
> **Highlights:** Striking rock formations.
> **Distance:** 1⁷⁄₁₀ miles round-trip.
> **Degree of difficulty:** Easy.

Skull Rock Interpretive Trail is Joshua Tree National Park at its very best: a vast array of rock formations, a Joshua tree forest, the yucca-dotted desert open and wide.

Skull Rock itself is one of the many rocks in the area that appear to resemble human beings, dinosaurs, monsters, cathedrals, and castles.

Directions to trailhead: The hike begins in the Jumbo Rocks Campground. Drive into the campground and park at the signed trailhead near the Loop E entrance.

The walk: The first half of the hike is on a nature trail that provides an introduction to the park's flora, wildlife, and geology. Beyond Skull Rock, the path crosses the park road, continues past more fantastic rock monoliths, then loops back to the campground entrance.

Queen Valley

California Riding and Hiking Trail

Terrain: Joshua tree–dotted valley.
Highlights: Wide-open spaces among park's namesake tree.
Distance: From Geology Tour Road to a ridgeline viewpoint
is 5 miles round-trip with 400-foot elevation gain.
Degree of difficulty: Moderate.

Joshua trees, thousands of them, thrive in Queen Valley, the scenic heart of the national park. With an elevation of about 4,000 feet, well-drained soil, and plenty of sun, the valley is an ideal habitat for the trees.

Mile after mile of Joshua trees dot the flat valley floor, which spreads south from Queen Mountain to a low divide separating it from Pleasant Valley. Queen Valley is backed by the Pinto Mountains to the east, the Little San Bernardino Mountains to the west and south, the Wonderland of Rocks and more mountains to the north.

This walk is a mellow ramble through wide-open, Joshua tree–dotted spaces on the California Riding and Hiking Trail.

Directions to trailhead: From Pinto Y-junction south of the park visitor center, fork right (west). In 5 miles, turn left (south) to Geology Tour Road. Drive 4½ miles until you reach the signed trailhead for the California Riding and Hiking Trail.

The walk: A short ramble west from Geology Tour Road brings you to mile marker 12. Your path heads west past juniper trees, then across the Joshua tree–sprinkled valley to mile marker 13.

The California Riding and Hiking Trail crests a ridge a few hundred yards past mile marker 14. Enjoy the expansive views of Queen Valley and the Little San Bernardino Mountains before returning the way you came.

Lost Horse Mine

Lost Horse Mine Trail

Terrain: Pinyon pine– and nolina-studded wash.
Highlights: Famous gold mine with colorful history.
Distance: To Lost Horse Mine is 3½ miles round-trip with
400-foot elevation gain.
Degree of difficulty: Moderate.

Lost Horse Mine was the most successful gold-mining operation in this part of the Mojave. More than 9,000 ounces of gold were processed from ore dug here in the late 1890s. The mine's 10-stamp mill still stands, along with a couple of large cyanide settling tanks and a huge winch used on the main shaft. The trail to the mine offers a close-up look at the remains of a colorful era and some fine views into the heart of the national park.

Many are the legends that swirl like the desert winds around the Lost Horse Mine. As the story goes, Johnny Lang in 1893 was camping in Pleasant Valley when his horse got loose. He tracked it out to the ranch belonging to Jim McHaney, who told Lang that his horse was "no longer lost" and threatened Lang's health and future.

Lang wandered over to the camp of fellow prospector Dutch Diebold, who told him that he had also been threatened by McHaney and his cowboys. A pity too, because he, Diebold, had discovered a promising gold prospect but had been unable to mark his claim's boundaries. After sneaking in to inspect the claim, Johnny Lang and his father, George, purchased all rights from Diebold for $1,000.

At first it looked like a bad investment, because McHaney's thugs prevented the Langs from reaching their claim. Partners came and went, and by 1895 Johnny Lang owned the mine with the Ryan brothers, Thomas and Jep.

Peak production years for the mine were 1896 through 1899. Gold ingots were hidden in a freight wagon and transported to Indio. The ruse fooled any would-be highwaymen.

But thievery of another sort plagued the Lost Horse Mine. The theft was of amalgam, lumps of quicksilver from which gold could later be separated. It seems that in this matter of amalgam, the mill's day shift, supervised by Jep Ryan, far outproduced the night shift, supervised by Lang. One of Ryan's men espied Lang stealing part of the amalgam. When Ryan gave Lang a choice—sell his share of the mine for $12,000 or go to the penitentiary—Lang sold out.

Alas, Johnny Lang came to a sad end. Apparently, his stolen and buried amalgam supported him for quite some time, but by the end of 1924, he was old, weak, and living in an isolated cabin. And hungry. He had shot and eaten his four burros and was forced to walk into town for food. He never made it. His partially mummified body, wrapped in a canvas sleeping bag, was found by prospector-rancher Bill Keys alongside present-day Keys View Road. He was buried where he fell.

Directions to trailhead: From the central part of Joshua Tree National Park, turn south from Cap Rock Junction onto Keys Road and drive 2½ miles. Turn left on a short dirt road. Here you'll find a park service interpretive display about Johnny Lang's checkered career. (You can also visit Lang's grave, located 100 feet north of the Lost Horse Mine turnoff on Keys Road.) The trail, a continuation of Lost Horse Mine Road, begins at a road barrier.

The walk: The trail, the old mine road, climbs above the left side of a wash. Pinyon pine and nolina dot the wash. Although the nolina is often mistaken for a yucca, its leaves are more flexible and its flowers smaller than those of yucca.

An alternative route for the first, or last, mile of this day hike is to walk from the parking area directly up the wash. The wash widens in about ¾-mile and forks; bear left and a short ascent will take you to the mine road. Turn right on the road and follow it to the mine.

A few open shafts remain near the Lost Horse, so be careful when you explore the mine ruins. Note the stone foundations opposite the mill site. A little village for the mine workers was built here in the late 1890s. Scramble up to the top of the hill above the mine for a panoramic view of Queen Valley, Pleasant Valley, and the desert ranges beyond.

Pushawalla Plateau
Pinyon Well Trail

Terrain: Canyon, Joshua tree–dotted Pushawalla Plateau.
Highlights: Historic Pinyon Well; vistas from atop plateau.
Distance: From parking area to Pinyon Well site is 1½ miles
round-trip; to Pushawalla Plateau is 6½ miles round-trip
with 1,500-foot elevation gain.
Degree of difficulty: Moderate to strenuous.

Water, especially in the desert where there is so little of it, is the
very essence of life. Pinyon Well was one such life-giving source, a
critical water supply for teamsters, miners, and their families.

During the 1890s, prospectors constructed a crude arrasta, then a
more elaborate stamp mill at Pinyon Well in order to extract gold
from ore dug at the Lost Horse, the Desert Queen, and other nearby
mines. Teamsters guided their wagons through Pushawalla Canyon
to Pinyon Well.

At the turn of the century, Pinyon Well was a little mining hamlet, a community that included women and children—an unusual
state of affairs. In later years, Pinyon Well's valuable water was
piped to the Piute Basin, serving mining operations there until the
early 1930s.

Pinyon Well put a gleam in the eye of one 1920s developer, who
envisioned a resort community rising from the wide-open spaces.
Pinyon Well, however, could not provide sufficient water to become
another Palm Springs.

This hike, which follows traces of the old road, visits Pinyon
Well, where water still seeps and attracts birds and wildlife. Past
the well, the trail ascends Pushawalla Plateau for excellent views of
the Coachella Valley and Palm Springs.

Directions to trailhead: Follow the Geology Tour Road 9½ miles
to the signed Pinyon Well turnoff.

The walk: The trail leads up-canyon ¾-mile to Pinyon Well.
Some cement tanks, rusty pipe, and foundations of old cabins mark
the site of Pinyon Well. It all seems a bit forlorn now—somehow,
it's easier to imagine teamsters swearing at their mules than to en-
vision happy families once living here.

The path continues with the canyon another ¾-mile and forks left. In another ¼-mile the canyon turns south, but you stay to the right with the somewhat faint road. A little farther along, the road becomes steeper and rockier as it climbs to Pushawalla Plateau. Atop the broad, pinyon pine– and Joshua tree–covered plateau is a view of Mount San Jacinto and some of the northern valleys and ranges of the park.

A trail continues some 8 more miles over the plateau and the crest of the Little San Bernardino Mountains all the way out to Dillon Road in Desert Hot Springs.

Pinto Basin Sand Dunes

Pinto Basin Trail

> **Terrain:** Stark, creosote-dotted basin, low sand dunes.
> **Highlights:** An emptiness that inspires; early human occupation of area.
> **Distance:** To sand dunes is 2 miles or so round-trip.
> **Degree of difficulty:** Easy.

As a habitat for human beings, Pinto Basin is, to say the least, forbidding: a barren lowland surrounded by austere mountains and punctuated by sand dunes. Nevertheless, some 2,000 to 4,000 years ago, native people lived here. Environmental conditions were friendlier then—creeks flowed across the center of the basin and a forest cloaked the mountainsides.

Still, even in those better times, the people who lived here made some successful adaptations to desert living and forged some specialized tools; anthropologists have named these unique ancients "Pinto Man." Elizabeth Campbell, a gifted amateur archaeologist from Twentynine Palms, began recovering artifacts from the Pinto Basin in the 1930s. Since then, evidence of Pinto Man culture has been found in other widely scattered parts of the California desert.

While today's visitor has difficulty imagining how even the most adaptive hunter-gatherers could have survived in the harsh environs of the Pinto Basin, real estate developers of the 1920s were not at all discouraged by the forbidding land and began selling parcels for homes and ranches. The Lake County Development Syndicate promised would-be buyers that an investment in Pinto Basin real estate would soon pay off big—as soon as a water source was developed. The water never came, of course, and the Depression of the 1930s ended the developers' scheme.

The walk to Pinto Basin's sand dunes begins at Turkey Flat, the site of an unsuccessful poultry farm in the 1920s. For experienced, well-conditioned hikers, Turkey Flat is the departure point for the climb of 3,983-foot Pinto Mountain, which lords it over the north side of the basin. Three routes, 9 to 13 miles round-trip, ascend washes, then tackle the shoulders of the peak.

Directions to trailhead: This walk begins from the Turkey Flat Trailhead off Pinto Basin Road, 5 miles east of Ocotillo Patch and 12 miles west of the junction with Old Dale Road.

The walk: The mellow ramble to the dunes, bedecked in spring with lilies and other wildflowers, is one for the whole family. From the parking area, head northeast to the low sandy ridge. Frolic in the sand until tired and return the same way.

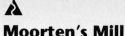

Moorten's Mill

Moorten's Mill Trail

Terrain: Cottonwood canyon.
Highlights: Historic mill, road.
Distance: 1 mile round-trip.
Degree of difficulty: Easy.

During the 1930s, "Cactus" Slim Moorten operated a stamp mill that processed ore from mines in the Cottonwood Spring area. After his mining days were over, Moorten turned desert landscaper and developed a reputation for locating and transplanting exotic cactus species during the worldwide cactus craze of the early 1950s. Moorten and his wife, Patricia, founded Moorten's Botanical Garden in Palm Springs.

Except for some building foundations and rusted tanks, not much remains of the mill site; however, another historical attraction nearby invites a visit.

In the early 1900s, teamsters drove their wagons over a stretch of nasty road near Cottonwood Spring known as Little Chilkoot Pass, a comparison to the infamous divide that faced Yukon prospectors on the way to the Klondike goldfields in 1898. The pass—a bypass, really—was built to get over a low cliff in a wash. Even by 1906 accounts, it was clear that this so-called shortcut wasn't; heavily laden ore wagons and their teams found passage extremely difficult. Misuse of public funds and moronic engineering were two common complaints about the pass, while the reaction of teamsters to this road cannot be printed here.

Directions to trailhead: Entering the national park from the south (via Interstate 10), travel 8 miles north of the park boundary to Cottonwood Spring Campground. Park at the Cottonwood Spring day-use area.

The walk: Follow the wash downstream from the Cottonwood Spring campground. The wash walk is marked with posts.

Cottonwood Canyon soon narrows and you pass below high, cactus-dotted rock walls. Next is the Little Chilkoot Pass; digging it with hand tools must have been quite an ordeal. Beyond the pass are the ruins of Moorten's Mill.

Mastodon Peak and Mastodon Mine

Mastodon Peak Trail

Terrain: Cottonwood-lined oasis, rocky peak.
Highlights: Cottonwood Spring, historic mining site, good vistas.
Distance: 3-mile loop trail with 400-foot elevation gain.
Degree of difficulty: Easy to moderate.

Mastodon Peak Trail packs a lot of sightseeing into a 3-mile walk: a cottonwood-shaded oasis, a gold mine, and a grand desert view.

Mastodon Peak, named by early prospectors for its behemothlike profile, was the site of the Mastodon Mine, a gold mine worked intermittently from 1919 to 1932. The ore was of high quality; however, the main ore body was cut off by a fault.

A mile down the trail from the mine is Winona, where some concrete foundations remain to mark the former mill and little town. Winona was home to workers at the Mastodon Mine, as well as workers at the mill, which processed ore from a number of nearby mines.

Views from elephantine-shaped Mastodon Peak include the Cottonwood Spring area and the Eagle Mountains. Clear-day panoramas extend from Mount San Jacinto above Palm Springs to the Salton Sea.

Directions to trailhead: Entering the national park from the south (via Interstate 10), travel 8 miles north of the park boundary to Cottonwood Spring Campground. Park at the Cottonwood Spring day-use area.

The walk: From the parking area, the path proceeds immediately to Cottonwood Spring, a collection of cottonwoods, California fan palms, and cattails crowded around a trickling spring.

The path continues ½-mile, following a wash to a junction. Lost Palms Trail heads right, but you take the left fork to ascend Mastodon Peak. A short spur trail leads to the summit. Enjoy views stretching from Cottonwood Campground just below to the Coachella Valley beyond.

The main trail descends to the shafts and ruins of Mastodon Mine. Another mile of travel brings you to Winona. Some shady trees—

including eucalyptus planted by miners—offer a pleasant rest stop. A last ¼-mile brings you to a fork in the road. The right fork leads to the campground; the left fork returns to Cottonwood Spring parking lot.

Lost Palms Oasis

Lost Palms Oasis Trail

Terrain: Washes, palm oases.

Highlights: Nature trail, hidden gem of a palm oasis.

Distance: From Cottonwood Spring Campground to Lost Palms Oasis is 8 miles round-trip with 300-foot elevation gain.

Degree of difficulty: Moderate.

Season: October to May.

Lost Palms Oasis Trail passes through a cactus garden, crosses a number of desert washes, and takes you to the two southern oases in the national park: Cottonwood and Lost Palms.

Largely man-made Cottonwood Spring Oasis was a popular overnight stop for freight haulers and prospectors during the mining years of 1870 to 1910. Travelers and teamsters journeying from Banning to the Dale Goldfield east of Twentynine Palms rested at the oasis.

Lost Palms Oasis is a hidden gem. Nearly a hundred palms are found in the deep canyon, whose steep igneous walls sparkle in the desert sun.

Directions to trailhead: From the south end of Joshua Tree National Park, follow the park road 8 miles to Cottonwood Spring Campground. Park your car at the campground. The trailhead is at the end of the campground.

The walk: Leaving Cottonwood Spring Campground, the trail ambles through a low desert environment of green-trunked paloverde, ironwood, and cottonwood trees, spindly ocotillo plants, and cholla cactus. Park service identification plaques describe the area's flora and fauna.

The trail, a bit difficult to follow through the sandy wash, brings you to Cottonwood Spring Oasis in ½-mile. Cottonwood Spring is home to a wide variety of birds and a large number of bees.

From Cottonwood Spring, the trail marches over sandy hills, past heaps of huge rocks, and along sandy draws and washes. A number of park service signs point the way at possibly confusing junctions. Finally, you rise above the washes and climb to a rocky outcropping overlooking the canyon harboring Lost Palms Oasis. From the overlook, descend the steep path around the boulders to the palms.

Little surface water is present at Lost Palms Oasis, but enough is underground for the palms to remain healthy. Lost Palms remained relatively untouched throughout the mining years, though some of its water was pumped to settlements eight miles to the south at Chiriaco Summit. Adjacent to Lost Palms Canyon is a handsome upper canyon called Dike Springs.

Shy and reclusive desert bighorn sheep are often seen around this oasis—particularly in hot weather when they need water more often.

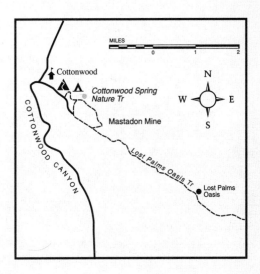

Anza-Borrego Desert State Park—California's largest.

5. Anza-Borrego Desert State Park

When Butterfield Overland stagecoaches sped from St. Louis through the Colorado Desert toward Pueblo de Los Angeles in the 1850s, the serpentine canyons and jagged mountains that are now part of Anza-Borrego Desert State Park stood as the last obstacle to the trip across the continent. Stagecoach passengers were only too happy to leave behind this vast, desolate wilderness. Since the 1930s, however, when 500,000 acres of palm oases, cactus flats, and fantastic badlands were preserved in a state park, this very vastness and desolation have attracted visitors.

East–west Highway 78 crosses the state park and reveals a land as intriguing as its names: Earthquake Valley, Grapevine Hills, Nude Wash. And Angelina Spring, Narrows Earth Trail, and Burro Bend. At Yaqui Well grow the spiny ironwood trees, and at Split Canyon you can see those botanical oddities, the puffy-looking elephant trees. At Split Mountain the road penetrates the middle of the mountain and offers an inside-out look at hundreds of sedimentary layers of ancient sea bottoms and fossil shell reefs.

Another long desert highway, S–22, the Salton Sea Parkway, also crosses the park from east to west. In 1929 Alfred "Doc" Beatty led a mule-drawn Fresno scraper through the Borrego Badlands to the Truckhaven Cafe on old Highway 99. Truckhaven Trail became a popular jeep road after World War II. When Highway S–22 was built in 1968 it followed Doc's road closely for much of its length. S–22 offers access to lonely Seventeen Palms Canyon, where a desert seep enables a group of fan palms to survive, and to the twisted sandstone formations of Calcite Canyon, where calcite, useful for making gun sights, was mined during World War II.

S–22, like a good many desert roads, has over the past 50 years evolved from trail to jeep road to highway. But if Colorado Desert roads have changed a great deal in the last half-century, desert vistas have not. One of my favorite views is off S–22 at Font's Point, where an overlook offers a breathtakingly beautiful panorama of Baja California, the Salton Sea, Borrego Valley, and the sculptured maze of the Borrego Badlands. This view has remained exactly the same as it was in the 1930s when *Los Angeles Times* outdoors writer Lynn J. Rogers stepped out of his Chevrolet and observed: "A myriad of furrowed canyons drop down into a wild confusion of tumbled gorges and pinnacles. Beyond is spread the great bowl of the Borrego Valley with scattered clearings and patches of brown mesquite stretched out in the aching clearness of the desert morning light."

Anza-Borrego Desert State Park includes virtually every feature that visitors associate with a desert: washes, badlands, mesas, palm oases, and much more. This diverse desert park boasts more than 20 palm groves, as well as year-round creeks, great stands of cholla and elephant trees, slot canyons, and badland formations.

Anza-Borrego is diverse, and it is huge: more than three times the size of Zion National Park. The 600,000-acre park stretches almost the whole length of San Diego County's eastern border between Riverside County and Mexico. Its elevation ranges from 100 feet below sea level near the Salton Sea to 6,000 feet above sea level atop San Ysidro Mountain.

California's largest state park preserves a 60-mile long, 30-mile-wide stretch of Colorado Desert from the Santa Rosa Mountains to the Mexican border. Lower in elevation than the Mojave Desert, the Colorado Desert is also hotter and drier. (The Colorado Desert in the extreme southeastern portion of California is only a small part of the larger Sonoran Desert, which covers about 120,000 acres of the American Southwest.)

The park, set aside in 1933, is named for the Mexican explorer Juan Bautista de Anza and the Spanish word for bighorn sheep, *borrego*. De Anza traversed the area in 1774, and the bighorn sheep still roam this land.

Travelers are welcomed to Anza-Borrego by what is probably the best visitor center in the state park system. Numerous self-guided nature trails and automobile tours allow visitors to set their own pace. An active natural history association and foundation sponsors many regularly scheduled ranger- and naturalist-led activities.

While the park is oriented to exploration by vehicle, a number of fine hikes await the desert trekker. A note to the uninitiated: hiking in this section of the Colorado Desert is guaranteed to make a desert rat out of anyone.

Among the sights are Calcite Canyon, where nature's cutting tools, wind and water, have shaped the ageless sandstone into steep, bizarre formations. The elephant tree grove is another strange sight. The trees' surreal colors, parchmentlike bark, and elephantine trunks are something to behold.

Coyote Canyon

Horse Camp, Ocotillo Flat, Lower Willows Trails

Terrain: Long, lush perennial creek.
Highlights: Magnificent ocotillo, great birding.
Distance: From Horse Camp to Lower Willows is 8 miles round-trip.
Degree of difficulty: Moderate to strenuous.
Precautions: Road into Coyote Canyon is four-wheel-drive only.

Hikers and horseback riders are attracted to Coyote Canyon and its numerous tributary canyons by springs, California fan-palm groves, and a variety of historical and archaeological features. Year-round Coyote Creek gives life to the state park's lushest riparian area— three willow-lined oases known as Lower, Middle, and Upper Willows.

In 1774 pathfinder Juan Bautista de Anza led soldiers and settlers through this earthquake-fractured gap between the Santa Rosa and San Ysidro mountains on their journey from Sonora, Mexico, to Monterey.

In the 20th century, road boosters periodically proposed constructing a paved highway from the northern edge of Borrego Valley to the town of Anza in Riverside County. Each time the paving proposal surfaced, it was thwarted by conservationists, and today the only road that penetrates Coyote Canyon is a primitive, 1930s-vintage jeep road.

Getting into Coyote Canyon, at least by auto, is definitely not half the fun. Be warned: wicked drop-offs, soft sand, and big rocks make this route impassable for standard autos and challenging even for four-wheel-drive enthusiasts.

While a few four-wheel drivers will take Coyote Canyon Road as a challenge, and will regard the warnings of state park rangers as a further challenge, the prudent will inquire about the latest road conditions and consider beginning their hikes at the two trailheads accessible to two-wheel-drive vehicles. These two trailheads are at the road's first crossing of Coyote Creek and at the Vern Whitaker Horse Camp.

Coyote Canyon's trail system was developed by park volunteer Vern Whitaker and is popular with both equestrians and hikers. White poles with yellow tops intermittently mark trails.

Some Coyote Canyon paths are closed between June 15 and September 15 to protect the water-seeking bighorn sheep who frequent the canyon during the summer.

Directions to trailhead: Drive 3½ miles north of the Christmas Circle to the intersection of Borrego Springs Road and Henderson Canyon Road. Turn north off the pavement onto dirt Horse Camp Road. After 3½ miles, the road forks. Continue another ¼-mile straight ahead to the Vernon V. Whitaker Horse Camp. (The right fork, often washed out, is a park service road only– no public use; it continues 1 mile to the first crossing of Coyote Creek.)

Another way to the Willows Creek trailhead is via DiGiorgio Road (four-wheel-drive and/or high-clearance vehicles advised by state park). Expect to encounter lots of soft sand on the road to Desert Gardens, then a very large drop-off at the first crossing of Coyote Creek, followed by deep ruts with steep climbs in and out of the creek at the second crossing. Lower Willows trailhead at the third crossing is the stopping point for many in four-wheel-drive vehicles, though it is possible to continue up-canyon on rugged Bypass Road. (It's 5⅗ miles from the end of the pavement to the Sheep Canyon trailhead sign. See Sheep Canyon walk.)

The walk: At Horse Camp join the flat open trail leading north. Soft sand churned by horses' hooves slows your gait. Two miles of travel brings you to the Coyote Creek ford known as Second Crossing, where there's a parking area for motorists not wishing to chance the creek crossing and a small metal utility building housing a creek-gauging station. Cross the creek here and either follow the four-wheel-drive road northwest or pick your own way between the cholla and ocotillo over flat open ground, staying between the creek bed and the road heading northwest. A 10-minute walk brings you to the intersection of the creek and the road at a park gate. This is the "sheep gate," which closes the road during the summertime so that bighorn sheep can reach water. A rock marker describes the sheep habitat. On the north side of the road is the signed junction with Ocotillo Flat Trail.

Continue past the gate and head northwest, following either the creek or walking the dirt road another ⅕-mile to Coyote Creek's Third Crossing.

Join signed Lower Willows Trail, a former jeep road, now a level packed-sand trail. The well-marked path, crowded by tamarisk and willow, heads northwest up the creek. You'll encounter a particularly lush and overgrown stretch of trail near Santa Catarina Spring, a major source of Coyote Creek's year-round water supply.

After 2 miles (4 miles from the trailhead), Lower Willows Trail Loop bears left (southwest) at a signed intersection with Main Wash Trail. Main Wash Trail continues northwest (right) toward Middle Willows, but you follow Willows Trail southwest across the center of the broad flood wash of Coyote Creek. After ¼-mile, your path intersects Coyote Canyon Jeep Road/Bypass Road. Turn left (south) on this road.

After ¼-mile, you'll pass the Sheep Canyon Jeep Road, which heads west to Sheep and Indian canyons, and after another ½-mile, you'll pass the signed Sheep Canyon trailhead marker on your right. This trail also heads west—to Sheep, Indian, and Cougar canyons. After yet another ½-mile, look left (north) for the spur road to the Santa Catarina Spring Historic Marker and spring overview. A short detour yield a nice view of the spring and Lower Willows.

You can hike a last mile southeast on Jeep Road/Bypass Road back to the trailhead, but use caution because the four-wheelers have limited visibility. A narrow trail has been constructed off the roadside to help keep vehicles and pedestrians separate.

Better yet, finish this figure-eight hike by joining Ocotillo Flat Trail, which leads a bit more than a mile through a cornucopia of cacti—cholla, fishhook, and beavertail—as well as one of the finest stands of ocotillo in California. On the north side of Ocotillo Flat are some dramatic sandstone formations known as the Coyote Canyon Badlands.

The path crosses the two Coyote Canyon roads and swings west back to the horse camp.

Sheep Canyon

Sheep Canyon Trail

> **Terrain:** Steep, lush canyon.
> **Highlights:** Cool grottoes, streamside relaxation.
> **Distance:** From Bypass Road to Sheep Canyon is 8 miles round-trip with 1,200-foot elevation gain; from Primitive Camp into Sheep Canyon is 4 miles round-trip.
> **Degree of difficulty:** Moderate to strenuous.

Sheep Canyon, a tributary of Coyote Canyon, welcomes the intrepid hiker with a seasonal stream lined with sycamores and cottonwood. Rugged and remote, the wilderness canyon is an excellent destination for a weekend backpacking trip.

Getting to the beginning of this hike is not easy. Driving to the trailhead on the four-wheel-drive road is difficult. (See the Coyote Canyon/Lower Willows walk.) The walking from Vernon V. Whitaker Horse Camp is easy, but there's lots of it—about 6½ miles one way.

Intrepid four-wheelers can begin this hike at the signed Sheep Canyon Trail located off Bypass Road, or continue by rough road all the way to Sheep Canyon Primitive Camp.

From the camp, a primitive path leads along the creek to a handsome rock-bound bowl.

Directions to trailhead: It is 13 miles from the Christmas Circle (8 miles from the end of the paved road) to the turnoff to Sheep Canyon. Turn left (west) off Bypass Road and drive 1⁷⁄₁₀ miles to a signed fork. Turn left (southwest) and drive ½-mile to Sheep Canyon Primitive Camp.

The walk: If you begin at Bypass Road, you'll join the path signed with symbols for "Equestrians/Pedestrians Only" and follow the sandy trail 1½ miles to Sheep Canyon Road. Bear left on the road, soon passing a right-forking road that leads back to Bypass Road. A ½-mile's walk brings you to Sheep Canyon Primitive Camp.

From the west end of the camp, head up the canyon along the creek bed, often filled with water in winter and spring. Stay to your right (north) and follow the main canyon. You'll find a sycamore-shaded pool about ⅓-mile up the canyon.

(The canyon's left branch, the south fork of Sheep Canyon, is very rugged. A rewarding side trip for hardy hikers is the rock scramble to the first palm grove.)

A ½-mile along, you'll visit a palm grove and a little grotto, then crisscross the creek a couple of times. At a mile out, cottonwoods make an appearance, and pools and flat granite slabs suggest a picnic. At 1½ miles, the canyon bends sharply west.

After another ½-mile's travel, you'll enter a bowl where several canyon tributaries converge. The bowl can be either a turnaround point or an invitation to study your topographic map and explore some mighty difficult terrain.

One of the grandest sights you'll ever glimpse in the desert—the reclusive bighorn sheep.

Cougar Canyon

Cougar Canyon Trail

> **Terrain:** Rugged, boulder-strewn canyon dotted with cotton-woods, sycamores, and palms.
> **Highlights:** Pool, waterfall.
> **Distance:** 3 miles round-trip with 800-foot elevation gain.
> **Degree of difficulty:** Moderate.

If, by means of some skilled four-wheeling or heroic hiking, you manage to reach the trailhead early in the day, you can explore both Sheep Canyon (see the walk) and Cougar Canyon in the same day. Cougar Canyon's short length is definitely worth the lengthy effort needed to visit it.

Caves, cascades, and water-polished boulders are the main attractions of this rugged canyon. Cougar, a fork of Indian Canyon, was a longtime seasonal camp of the Cahuilla, as evidenced by bedrock mortars and caves found in the canyon. A rock cave at the north edge of the canyon mouth is believed to have been used as a *temescal,* or sweat house.

Directions to trailhead: This walk begins at the road leading to Sheep Canyon Primitive Camp. The trail is a closed road (the old Indian Canyon jeep road) going south from the mouth of Sheep Canyon.

It is 13 miles from the Christmas Circle (8 miles from the end of the paved road) to the turnoff to Sheep Canyon. Turn left (west) off Bypass Road and drive 1$\frac{7}{10}$ miles to a signed fork. Turn left (south-west) and drive a ½-mile to Sheep Canyon Primitive Camp.

The walk: Head south along the old eroded jeep road. The path crosses Cougar Canyon's creek bed a couple of times as it ascends the alluvial fan (*bajada*). About ¾-mile from the trailhead, you'll reach the canyon mouth. Look for the rock cave the Cahuilla used for a sweat house on a ledge above the creek.

Soon after the trail enters the canyon, you'll join the rough path on the north side of the creek. At first, you'll travel some 50 feet above the creek, but soon Cougar Canyon narrows, forcing you to descend to the rocky creek bed.

At 1¼ miles from the trailhead is a palm grove on the left bank. You'll continue on a faint trail along the south canyon wall to a point overlooking a pool and waterfall.

Pick your way through the cottonwood trees and granite rocks to the 20-foot waterfall and the deep pool below it. Traveling any farther up-canyon requires technical rock-climbing skills, so after enjoying this tranquil place, return the way you came.

Borrego Palm Canyon

Borrego Palm Canyon Trail

> **Terrain:** Palm oasis in rocky gorge.
> **Highlights:** California's third-largest palm oasis.
> **Distance:** To the waterfall is 3 miles round-trip with 600-foot elevation gain; to South Fork is 6½ miles round-trip with 1,400-foot gain.
> **Degree of difficulty:** Moderate.

Borrego Palm Canyon is the third-largest palm oasis in California, and the first site sought for a desert state park back in the 1920s. It's a beautiful, well-watered oasis tucked away in a rocky V-shaped gorge.

The trail visits the first palm grove and a waterfall. A longer option takes you exploring farther up-canyon. In winter, the trail to the falls is one of the most popular in the park. In summer, you'll have the oasis all to yourself. Watch for bighorn sheep, which frequently visit the canyon.

Directions to trailhead: The trail begins at Borrego Palm Canyon Campground, located 1 mile north of park headquarters. Trailhead parking is available at the west end of the campground near the campfire circle.

The walk: Beginning at the pupfish pond, you walk up-canyon past many desert plants that provided food and shelter for Native Americans. Willow was used for home building and bow making; brittlebush and creosote were valued for their healing qualities; honey, along with mesquite and beavertail cactus, was a food staple. You may also notice shallow Indian grinding holes in the granite.

The broad alluvial fan at the mouth of the canyon narrows, and sheer rock walls soon enclose you as the trail continues along the healthy, but seasonal stream. Already surprised to learn how an apparently lifeless canyon could provide all the Native Americans' necessary survival ingredients, you're surprised once more when Borrego Palm Oasis comes into view. Just beyond the first group of palms is a damp grotto where a waterfall cascades over huge boulders. The grotto is a popular picnic area and rest stop.

From the falls, you may take an alternate trail back to the campground. This trail travels along the south side of the creek, past some magnificent ocotillos, and gives you a different perspective on this unique desert environment. By following the optional route, you can continue hiking up the canyon. Hiking is more difficult up-canyon after the falls, with lots of dense undergrowth and boulders to navigate around.

To South Fork: From the "tourist turnaround" continue up the canyon. The creek's fairly dependable water supply is usually running late in the fall. This makes the canyon wet, so watch your footing on the slippery, fallen palm fronds. The canyon narrows even more and the trail dwindles to nothing. Parallel the streambed and boulder-hop back and forth across the water. The canyon zigs and zags quite a bit, so you can never see much more than a few hundred yards ahead. The hike is well worth the effort, though, because most of the 800 or so palms in the canyon are found in its upper reaches. Sometimes you'll spot rock climbers practicing their holds on the steep red-rock cliffs above you.

At 1¾ miles from the falls, the canyon splits. Straight ahead, to the southwest, is South Fork. The rocky gorge of South Fork, smothered with bamboo, possesses all the canyon's water. It's quite difficult to negotiate. South Fork ascends to the upper slopes of San Ysidro Mountain (6,417 feet). The Middle Fork (the way you came) of Borrego Palm Canyon is dry and more passable. It's possible to hike quite a distance first up Middle Fork, then up North Fork of Borrego Palm Canyon, but check with park rangers first. It's extremely rugged terrain.

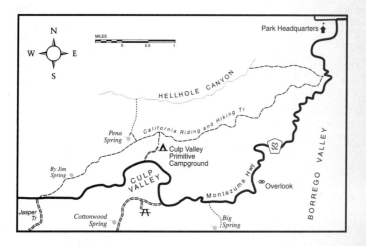

San Ysidro Mountain
Panorama Overlook Trail

Terrain: Rocky ridge of San Ysidro Mountain.
Highlights: Good overview of visitor center area.
Distance: 1 mile round-trip from Borrego Palm Canyon
  Campground; 2 miles round-trip from visitor center.
Degree of difficulty: Easy.

Panorama Overlook Trail delivers what it promises: vistas of the Borrego Valley and Borrego Badlands, the Vallecito Mountains and the Santa Rosa Mountains. Take this walk at dawn and you'll enjoy watching the rising sun chase shadows from the many mountains and canyons below the overlook. Bring along a park map to identify the considerable geography at your feet. A state park trail second in popularity only to Borrego Palm Canyon Nature Trail, the path is a good one for getting the lay of the land before embarking on more strenuous and far-reaching Anza-Borrego explorations.

One such (extremely) strenuous exploration begins where Panorama Overlook Trail ends. Experienced desert hikers in top form may continue up the trailless shoulder of San Ysidro Mountain past

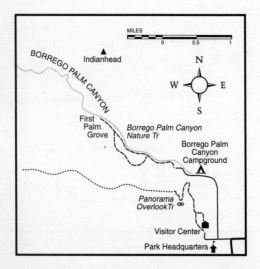

giant boulders, cacti, shrubs, and junipers to the mile-high top of the mountain. It's only a 7-mile round-trip, but a brutal 4,400-foot gain and an all-day hike to the mile-high summit. The panoramic views from the peak are magnificent.

Before hitting the trail, check out the nature and history exhibits at the park visitor center. You can start walking from the visitor center on the signed, ½-mile-long Campground Trail or from a trailhead in the Borrego Palm Canyon Campground.

Directions to trailhead: Anza-Borrego Desert State Park Visitor Center is located on Palm Canyon Drive just west of Highway S–22 in Borrego Springs. You can park in the visitor center lot (sometimes crowded on the weekends), but rangers ask that you help ease congestion by continuing up the road into the campground (day-use fee required). Ignore the many signs pointing toward Borrego Palm Canyon Nature Trail and proceed to the trailhead parking area near campsite 71.

Hellhole Canyon

Hellhole Canyon Trail

Terrain: Lush canyon amid arid desert.
Highlights: Fern-filled grotto, waterfall.
Distance: From County Road S–22 to Maidenhair Falls
   is 5 miles round-trip with 900-foot elevation gain.
Degree of difficulty: Moderate.

Add Hellhole Canyon to the list of great geographical misnomers. Just as Greenland is anything but green, Hellhole Canyon is far from, well . . . hellish. Cottonwoods, California fan palms, ferns, and mosses thrive in the canyon, which hosts a blissful waterfall.

Certainly this hike's destination—Maidenhair Falls—is no misnomer. Maidenhair ferns enshroud the 30-foot-high falls. The presence of a lush, fern-filled grotto in the midst of one of the West's most parched landscapes is a small miracle, an example of nature's mysterious ways.

Not only is Hellhole Canyon attractive, it's convenient—just a few miles as the cactus wren flies from the Anza-Borrego Desert State Park Visitor Center.

An intermittent trail travels through the long and deep canyon. Caution: While the canyon's riparian growth is easy on the eye, it's difficult to penetrate; expect slow-going through the thick vegetation.

You may begin your trek to Hellhole Canyon from the park visitor center or from a trailhead located just off S–22. I recommend the latter, which shaves a mile from the hike and avoids the sometimes congested visitor center parking lot.

Directions to trailhead: From its intersection with Palm Canyon Drive, proceed ⁷⁄₁₀-mile southwest on Montezuma Valley Road to the parking area on the right (west) side of the road. A bulletin board features trail and nature information.

The walk: Follow the signed California Riding and Hiking Trail some 200 yards to a junction; the riding and hiking trail splits left, while you bear right, heading southwest over the broad alluvial fan. The well-defined sandy trail crosses a desert garden of cholla, creosote bush, desert lavender, and ocotillo.

A bit more than a mile out, the path angles toward the mouth of Hellhole Canyon, distinguished by riparian trees and palms and looking altogether different from that smaller, drier tributary canyon to its right (north). The trail stays to the left of the fan, as should the hiker until entering the mouth of the canyon.

Once in the canyon, you might find yourself walking next to a wet or dry (depending on the season) watercourse. Try to steer clear of the very bottom of the canyon, an obstacle course of brush, boulders, and fallen trees.

The thickening of the canyon's scattered palm groves and the narrowing of the canyon walls signal that you're nearing Maidenhair Falls.

Ultra-ambitious hikers can continue bushwhacking up Hellhole Canyon, but most travelers will be content to enjoy the soft light and tranquillity around the falls and then return to the trailhead.

⚠

Calcite Canyon

Calcite Canyon Trail

Terrain: Sandstone formations.
Highlights: Unusual nature- and human-shaped canyon.
Distance: From County Road S–22 to Calcite Mine is 4 miles round-trip with 500-foot elevation gain.
Degree of difficulty: Moderate.

Nature's cutting tools, wind and water, have shaped the ageless sandstone in Calcite Canyon into steep, bizarre formations. The cutting and polishing of the uplifted rock mass have exposed calcite crystals. Calcite is a common enough carbonate and found in many rocks, but only in a few places are the crystals so pure.

It was the existence of these crystals, with their unique refractive properties, that brought prospectors to this part of the desert. The jeep trail was built in the mid-1930s to give miners access to Calcite Canyon, as it came to be called. Because of the calcite crystals' excellent double-refraction properties, they were used in the manufacture of gun sights. Mining activity increased during World War II.

The calcite was taken from the canyon in long trenches, which look as if they were made yesterday. The desert takes a long time to heal.

The day hike follows the jeep road to its dead end at the mine. You'll see the Calcite Mine area up-close and get a good overlook of the many washes snaking toward the Salton Sea. A return trip through Palm Wash and its tributaries lets you squeeze between perpendicular walls and obtain a unique perspective on the forces that shape the desert sands. The awesome effects of flash flooding are easily discerned by the hiker and suggest that a narrow wash is the last place you want to be in a rainstorm.

Directions to trailhead: Follow County Road S–22 west from Highway 86, or 20 miles from the Christmas Circle, to Calcite Jeep Road. The jeep road is just west of a microwave tower.

The walk: Follow the jeep road, which first drops into the south fork of Palm Wash, then begins to climb northwest. Along the road you'll see long slots cut into the hillsides for the removal of calcite. Calcite Jeep Road dips a final time, then climbs a last ½-mile toward the mine. Two miles from the trailhead, the road ends at the mining area.

146

Calcite crystal fragments embedded in the canyon walls and scattered on the desert floor glitter in the sun. Behind the mining area, to the northeast, is a gargantuan hunk of white sandstone dubbed "Locomotive Rock." The imaginative can picture a great Baldwin locomotive chugging up a steep grade. If you look carefully, you'll be able to see Seventeen Palms and some of the palms tucked away in Palm Wash in a bird's-eye view of the east side of the state park.

You can return the same way or descend through tributaries of the middle fork of Palm Wash. Take a last look at the steep ravines and washes to get your bearings. Middle Fork is but a hop, skip, and jump from the mine, but the jump's a killer—a 50-foot plunge to a deep intersecting wash. To get into the wash, you need to descend ½-mile on Calcite Jeep Road to a small tributary wash. Go down this wash, which is fairly steep at first. The sandstone walls close in on you. One place, Fat Man's Misery, allows only one fat man (or two skinny day hikers) to squeeze through at a time. When you reach the middle fork, a prominent canyon, follow it about ¼-mile to the brief jeep trail connecting the wash to Calcite Road. Hike back up Calcite Road ⅒-mile to the parking area.

Calcite Canyon—gun sights and sights-to-see.

Tamarisk Grove Campground, Yaqui Pass

Kenyon Overlook, Cactus Loop, Yaqui Well Trails

Terrain: Cactus-covered slopes.
Highlights: Rich desert flora, excellent bird-watching at
Yaqui Well.
Distance: 1 to 2 miles each round-trip.
Degree of difficulty: Easy.

At the V-shaped highway junction where S–3 swings north toward
Borrego Valley from Highway 78 are a tumble of low ridges and
canyons, a campground, and a trio of nature trails. One path begins
atop Yaqui Pass; the other two begin opposite inviting Tamarisk
Grove Campground, a pleasant place to overnight or to picnic.

From Yaqui Pass, *Kenyon Overlook Trail* (1¼ miles round-trip)
leads ¼-mile to a viewpoint. Below sprawls the Mescal Bajada, one
of the largest *bajadas* (deltalike fans of gravel and silt) in the state
park. Mescal, or desert agave, is the dominant plant in the *bajada*.
Also visible are the Pinyon Mountains and, on clear days, the
Salton Sea.

The trail continues to a second overlook, then weaves ¾-mile
through a low desert flora of creosote bush, cactus, and jojoba to
undeveloped Yaqui Pass Campground and trail's end. Walk 200
yards along S–3 back to the trailhead.

Cactus Loop Trail (1 mile round-trip) ascends a rocky slope past
a diversity of cacti—beavertail, barrel, fishhook, and cholla. Most
spectacular are the 6-foot-high teddy-bear cholla.

Of all desert flora, the cholla has the most sinister reputation; its
evils have been repeatedly chronicled by Western writers. Joseph
Smeaton Chase in his 1919 classic, *California Desert Trails,* writes:
"First it certainly is in villainous traits and in the ill-regard of every
desert traveler. It is an ugly object 3 or 4 feet high, with stubby
arms standing out like amputated stumps. The older parts are usually black with decay, the rest of a sickly greenish white, and the
whole thing is covered with horrible barbed spines, uncountable in
quantity and detestable in every regard." Just to make sure the
reader fully understands his loathing for cholla, Chase adds in final

fulmination: "If the plant bears any helpful or even innocent part in the scheme of things on this planet, I should be glad to hear of it."

Yaqui Well Trail (2 miles round-trip) leads to a narrow waterfall that attracts birds and bird-watchers. Along the way, the cacti, as well as such characteristic desert flora as ocotillo, mesquite, and jojoba, are identified and described.

Ironwood, willow, and mesquite thrive around Yaqui Well, which attracts abundant wildlife. From nearby Yaqui Well Primitive Camp, you can join dirt Grapevine Canyon Road, which follows ironwood- and mesquite-lined San Felipe Creek. The road meets Highway S–3 just short of the trailhead.

Directions to trailhead: Bill Kenyon Trail begins at a signed trail-head atop Yaqui Pass on S–3, some 12½ miles from the park visitor center. Drive 1½ miles over the pass on S–3 to reach Tamarisk Grove Campground and the signed trailheads for Cactus Loop Trail and Yaqui Well Trail.

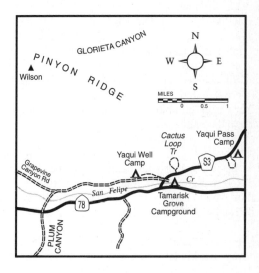

▲

Pinyon Ridge
Wilson Trail

Terrain: Pinyon pine–dotted ridge.
Highlights: Panoramic views.
Distance: 8½ miles round-trip with 1,400-foot elevation gain.
Degree of difficulty: Moderate to strenuous.

Pinyon Ridge is just that—a large block of boulders and pinyon pine standing just high enough above the desert floor to offer a 360-degree view. Its lower slopes are cloaked in cactus and creosote bush, its upper elevations dotted with yucca, chamise, and the pinyon pine promised by its name.

Pinyon Ridge and some of its environs are included in a state-designated wilderness area. Dirt roads abound, but the one climbing the ridge, an old jeep road, is closed to all but foot traffic.

Wilson Trail and Wilson Peak take their names from Borrego Valley cattle rancher Alfred Wilson, who grazed his cattle in these parts in the late-19th century. The trail gives out a bit before the summit, but a short, cross-country scramble will take you to the top. Rewarding the hiker's peak-climbing efforts are excellent views from Borrego Valley to the Salton Sea.

Your route to the trailhead—Culp Valley Road—can usually be traveled with two-wheel-drive vehicles; however, brush does crowd the road in places. Watch your paint job! If the road has deteriorated, or is too overgrown for your taste, numerous turnouts along the way allow you to leave your vehicle short of the trailhead. It's a nice 2-mile road walk from Cottonwood Spring to the Wilson trailhead.

Directions to trailhead: From Highway S–22 (Montezuma Highway) at mileage marker 10.4, turn west onto signed, dirt Culp Valley Road. At ⅔-mile, a spur road on the left (south) leads ⅓-mile to Culp Valley Picnic Area—a couple of tables beneath some shade trees offering a great view of Culp Valley's grassland floor.

At ⅗-mile, a right-branching spur road leads to a dead-end parking area for Culp Valley visitors.

A mile from the highway, after passing two more left-forking roads, you'll spot three large cottonwood trees standing near Cottonwood Spring, a pipe-fed concrete water basin; the overflow nurtures a patch of lush greenery.

After 2 more miles of travel on Culp Valley Road, you'll reach a small turnaround and the signed Wilson trailhead.

The walk: Wilson Trail heads southeast over hard-packed sand. The climb is through an intriguing mix of desert and mountain flora: cholla, yucca, and bearvertail cactus as well as manzanita, pinyon pine, and juniper.

The path winds south and east, passing boulders stacked upon boulders like a child's blocks.

Four miles along, the old road/trail ends, leaving you just north of Wilson Peak. Make your way between the boulders and weatherworn pinyon pine to the bench mark at the top of the peak.

The panoramic view includes the Laguna and Cuyamaca mountains to the southwest and the Santa Rosa Mountains to the northeast.

Harper Canyon

Harper Canyon Trail

Terrain: Canyon, natural bowl.
Highlights: A "desert garden," abundant ironwood trees.
Distance: 9 miles round-trip with 1,500-foot elevation gain.
Degree of difficulty: Moderate.

Cattle ranchers Julius and Amby Harper left their name on Harper Canyon, but a designation more evocative of its geography might be "Cactus Canyon" or "Ironwood Canyon."

The first mile of the hike passes a profusion of cacti known as the Cactus Garden. A half-dozen types of Colorado Desert cacti, especially barrel cactus, thrive here, along with ocotillo, smoke tree, desert lavender, and ironwood. Ironwood and the sweet-smelling, purple-blossomed desert lavender are abundant in Harper Canyon.

Harper Flat was heavily used by the Cahuilla people, who left behind many bedrock mortars and hand tools. In more modern times, the flat was used by off-highway vehicles, but it is now protected, along with much of the Pinyon Mountains, within a state park wilderness area.

Two-wheel-drive vehicles with high clearance can proceed as far as Kane Springs. Expect lots of ruts and some soft sand along the way. The route beyond Kane Springs Road is four-wheel-drive only.

The mileage and walk description assume that you don't have four-wheel drive and are hiking the first leg.

Directions to trailhead: From Highway 78, at the 87.2 mileage marker, turn south onto a signed dirt road and proceed 1½ miles to a T-intersection with Kane Springs Road. Turn right (west) and proceed ⅓-mile down a bumpy road to a jeep trail on your left. (Four-wheel-drive-only begins at this point.) From here, it's a 1½-mile journey (driving or walking) to road's end at the trailhead for Harper Canyon.

The walk: Your first mile of trail takes you past the Cactus Garden. Most noticeable are some basketball-sized barrel cacti.

About a mile out, be careful to stay on the road rather than straying up the wide tributary canyon to your right. (Such a detour—a scramble up the flanks of Sunset Peak for a 360-degree view—can be rewarding, however.)

After reaching road's end, you'll head south up a sandy wash, the main branch of Harper Canyon. The route is a mixture of sand by-ways and some boulder-hopping. Stick to the center of the wash and avoid tributary canyons branching both east and west.

A mile from Harper Flat, the canyon narrows; ½-mile away, the canyon opens up and levels out into a wide, willow-lined wash.

Climb a large mound of juniper-spiked boulders for a great view of Harper Flat and the mountains beyond.

▲
Blair Valley

Ghost Mountain, Morteros, Pictograph Trails

> **Terrain:** Bouldered ridges of Blair Valley.
> **Highlights:** Native rock art, an eccentric settler's homesite.
> **Distance:** ½-mile to 2½ miles each round-trip.
> **Degree of difficulty:** Easy to moderate.

Tucked between the high desert and low desert, between Whale Peak and Granite Mountain, is Blair Valley, an inviting locale for camping and hiking. Bouldered hills fringing the valley hide secluded campsites, and dirt roads and footpaths lead to cultural sites that offer a glimpse into the lives of the native Kumeyaay and the settlers who followed.

Getting to—and around—Blair Valley via Highway S–2 and two-wheel-drive-passable dirt roads is fairly easy these days. Not so in the stagecoach era, when the Butterfield Overland Mail wagons struggled across Blair Valley and over the high-desert passes. At the northern edge of the valley was a rocky incline known as Foot and Walker Pass; it was so steep that stage passengers were often forced to disembark and walk—even help push the stage— over the pass. Atop the pass is a monument commemorating the pioneers who came this way and an excellent vista of Blair Valley.

Before the settlers came, the native Kumeyaay camped in Blair Valley. They left behind *morteros* (grinding rocks) and pictographs (rock art), which today can be reached by short hikes.

In the 1930s Marshal South, his poet wife, Tanya, and their three children went native in a big way. They built an adobe house called Yaquitepec, collected rainwater in cisterns, cooked outdoors, and tried to live a very basic and natural life.

The ruins of Marshal South Cabin, as it's known, can also be reached by trail. *Ghost Mountain Trail* (2 miles round-trip with 400-foot elevation gain) climbs steep but well-graded switchbacks to the ruins of the Marshal South Cabin. Not much remains of the dwelling except for some walls and foundations, but the panoramic view is well worth the climb.

To reach the trailhead for the Marshal South Cabin, leave Highway S–2 at mileage marker 22.9 and turn east into Blair Valley. The dirt road passes many campsites as it travels 2⅖ miles to a signed junction. Bear right to "Ghost Mountain Trail" and drive ⅖-mile to road's end at the signed trail.

Return to the main road, then continue 1⅕ miles to the signed Morteros parking area. *Morteros Trail* (½-mile round-trip) leads to dozens of grinding holes in the boulders where Kumeyaay women pulverized seeds and pods such as chia and mesquite beans.

To reach the beginning of Pictograph Trail, continue ⅒ mile beyond the Morteros parking area to a junction. The left fork leads north to Little Blair Valley, then north to S–2. (This narrow, sandy route is iffy for two-wheel-drive vehicles; a safer bet back to the highway is the way you came.) Take the right fork and drive 1½ miles to the parking area.

Pictograph Trail (2½ miles round-trip with 500-foot elevation gain) ascends a pinyon pine– and juniper-dotted ridge, then descends and follows a sandy wash named Smuggler Canyon. About ¾-mile from the trailhead, look for the red-and-yellow-hued pictographs on the face of a large boulder on the right side of the canyon. From the pictographs, the path continues another ½-mile through the canyon, which narrows, then abruptly ends at a 200-foot drop-off. From the lip of a dry waterfall, carefully enjoy the good views.

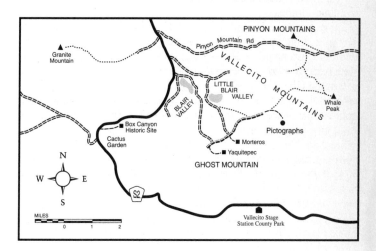

Elephant Trees

Elephant Trees Discovery Trail

Terrain: Alluvial fan.
Highlights: Odd elephant trees, intriguing interpretive trail.
Distance: 1½ miles round-trip with 100-foot elevation gain.
Degree of difficulty: Easy.

A rarity in California deserts, the odd elephant tree is much admired by visitors to Anza-Borrego Desert State Park. Its surreal color scheme (was this tree designed by committee?) of green foliage, red-tan twigs, yellow-green peeling parchmentlike bark, white flowers, and blue berries is something to behold. The stout trunk and the way the branches taper vaguely suggest an elephant, but lots of imagination is required.

The tree's aromatic red sap is related to frankincense and myrrh. Mayans and Aztecs burned the resin as incense and used the sap to dye their clothes.

Enjoy this hike by following the 1½-mile nature trail and/or by trekking along an alluvial fan to some elephant trees.

A herd estimated at 500 elephant trees grows at this end of the state park. *Birsera microphylla* is more common in Baja California and in the Gila Range of Arizona. (The elephant tree, along with all other park vegetation, is protected by state law.) The park has three populations of elephant trees, but the one off Split Mountain Road is the most significant.

Elephant Trees Discovery Trail, besides examining this botanical oddity, interprets various desert flora and geological features of this part of the Colorado Desert. An interpretive brochure, keyed to numbered posts along the trail, is available at the trailhead, from park rangers, and from the visitor center.

Directions to trailhead: From Ocotillo Wells (located about 40 miles west of Brawley and 78 miles east of Escondido on Highway 78), turn south on Split Mountain Road and proceed 6 miles to the signed turnoff for the Elephant Trees Area. Follow a dirt road 1 mile to the trailhead.

The walk: Follow the nature trail until signpost 10, where you'll see the first elephant tree on the hike.

Those experienced hikers who wish to see more elephant trees will leave the trail here and hike west up the broad alluvial fan. You'll encounter bits of trail, but really the route is cross-country. Keep the mountains on the western horizon in your sight. A mile's walk brings you to some elephant trees.

Return the way you came back to the nature trail, which follows the numbered posts through a dry streambed and loops back to the trailhead.

Visit a herd of elephants on this nature trail.

Agua Caliente County Park
Squaw Pond, Moonlight Canyon Trails

Terrain: Slopes and canyons of Tierra Blanca Mountains.
Highlights: Soak in hot springs, abundant desert flora.
Distance: 1½ to 2½ miles round-trip.
Degree of difficulty: Easy to moderate.

There's nothing like a good soak after a good hike. At Agua Caliente Springs in the middle of the Colorado Desert, you can have both—an inspiring walk and a soothing mineral bath.

A hot spring, along with a good-sized campground, a store, and the natural beauty of the Tierra Blanca Mountains, makes Agua Caliente County Park a popular weekend retreat. The park, open from Labor Day to Memorial Day, is especially delightful in March and April when usually abundant desert wildflowers splash color on the *blanca* (white) mountains behind the campground.

Seismic activity (an offshoot of the Elsinore Fault) that long ago shaped the surrounding mountains also boosted water to the surface to form the mineral springs. The natural springs in the area give life to mesquite, willows, and palms and also attract many animals and birds.

Centuries ago the native Kumeyaay bathed in the springs. The Spanish who followed dubbed the springs Agua Caliente, Hot Water. Generations of pioneers, prospectors, and desert travelers have found relaxation here.

Today's visitors can soak away their cares in a large, shallow outdoor pool geothermally heated to 96 degrees or in an indoor pool boosted to more than 100 degrees and equipped with Jacuzzi jets.

The park has 140 campsites, hot showers, a picnic area, a children's play area, and even spiffy shuffleboard courts. Surrounding the park is Anza-Borrego Desert State Park, California's largest.

Two trails explore the county park and visit undeveloped tiny springs (seeps) in the surrounding hills. Squaw Pond Trail leads to mesquite-filled Squaw Canyon; Moonlight Canyon Trail fulfills the promise of its name.

Squaw Pond Trail ascends a mesquite-dotted slope above the park's campfire circle and soon comes to a junction. Desert Overlook Trail branches left and climbs a steep ¼-mile to a panorama of the surrounding mountains. Ocotillo Ridge Trail, an abandoned nature trail, weaves through abundant desert flora and returns to the park entry road.

Continue on signed Squaw Pond Trail, which descends a draw lined with teddy-bear cholla and soon arrives at Squaw Pond, a boggy, willow-fringed area nurturing a single palm tree.

From the campground, *Moonlight Canyon Trail* ascends briefly but steeply to a rocky saddle, curves east, then descends into a narrow wash. After passing a willow-lined seep in the middle of the canyon, the trail circles back to the park campground.

Directions to trailhead: Agua Caliente County Park is located on Highway S–2 (the main north–south artery through Anza-Borrego Desert State Park), 22 miles southeast of Highway 78. Parking for Squaw Pond Trail is next to the park entry station (day-use fee) in a picnic area. Moonlight Canyon Trail begins at campsite 140 next to the shuffleboard courts.

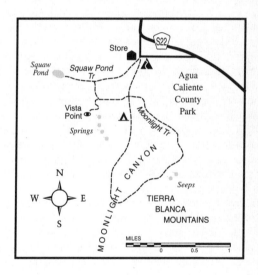

Mountain Palm Springs

Six Oa.ses Trail

> **Terrain:** Sandy washes, rocky canyons.
> **Highlights:** 6 palm oases.
> **Distance:** 2½ miles round-trip.
> **Degree of difficulty:** Easy.

At Mountain Palm Springs, half a dozen palm groves welcome the walker. These groves of California fan palms in the Tierra Blanca Mountains are less hidden than most others in the Colorado Desert; some are visible from the highway, and all can be visited on a mellow hike.

The palms are clustered in closely bunched communities within several narrow canyons. Abundant teddy-bear cholla and the occasional elephant tree grow on the canyon walls above the palms.

The palms all lie within 1 square mile of terrain, so the hiker gets a lot of palms per mile in a 2½-mile tour of Mountain Palm Springs.

Directions to trailhead: From Highway S–2 at mileage marker 47, some 54 miles from the park visitor center, turn west at the signed turnoff for Mountain Palm Springs. Follow the dirt road into the primitive campground and park at the trailhead.

The walk: From the parking area, 2 trails lead into the canyon. Begin on the main trail heading west and you'll soon reach some smallish palms in a rocky setting known as Pygmy Grove. At ¾-mile from the trailhead is Southwest Grove. (A side trail leads to Torote Bowl, where elephant trees grow.)

From Southwest Grove, one of the park's largest groves, look carefully for the northbound trail that leads over a rocky ridge to Surprise Canyon and its small palm grove. It's well worth the walk to travel up-canyon to lush Palm Bowl. The path down Surprise Canyon brings you within sight of North Grove and returns you to the trailhead.

Bow Willow and Rockhouse Canyons

Rockhouse Canyon Trail

> **Terrain:** Two desert canyons.
> **Highlights:** Historic rock house.
> **Distance:** From Bow Willow Campground to Rockhouse is
>   7 miles round-trip with 700-foot elevation gain.
> **Degree of difficulty:** Moderate.

This enjoyable day hike, for more experienced hikers, explores two intriguing canyons—Bow Willow and Rockhouse.

A turn-of-the-century miner, Nicolas Swartz, boasted that he took $18,000 worth of gold from his remote desert mine. In the great tradition of Lost Mine Legends, he died without leaving a map. In 1906 Swartz built a rock house in an anonymous canyon that soon picked up the name of his structure.

History is a muddled affair. There are two rock houses in the state park—and some question as to which actually belonged to Swartz. Some local historians believe that Swartz located his house in Nicolas Canyon on the other side of the park and say that the Darrel McCain family built the rock house in Rockhouse Canyon as a line shack for a cattle operation.

This looping trail takes you climbing through a single-palm canyon, visits the rock house and its canyon, and returns by way of the wash on the bottom of Bow Willow Canyon. Spring scatters color in the wash. Monkey flowers, desert stars, and a host of wildflowers brighten the sands and gravel bars. Even ocotillo changes its fit-only-for-firewood appearance and displays new green leaves and flaming red flowers.

Directions to trailhead: From Interstate 8 in Ocotillo, take County Road S–2 16 miles to the turnoff for Bow Willow Canyon and Campground. Follow the good hard-packed sand road 1½ miles to the campground. Park in the campground, but don't take a campsite someone could use.

The walk: Hike up Bow Willow Canyon on the signed jeep trail. Before you get much past the campground, make a 90-degree left turn (south) across a few hundred yards of wash to pick up the foot trail. A beleaguered young palm tree is ¼-mile up the trail. You begin climbing steadily through a desert garden of granite boulders, agave, and cholla cactus.

As you near Rockhouse Canyon, the trail descends briefly and intersects Rockhouse Canyon Jeep Trail. Follow the jeep trail west for 1 mile to Swartz's abandoned rock house. We can only pray that Swartz was a better prospector than architect. However, it's the only shade around, so this is no time to quibble over aesthetics.

From the rock house, you follow a tentative foot trail that drops down into Bow Willow Canyon. The wash on the canyon floor makes a unique hiking experience. In the wash, there's less of that relentless creosote that gives so much of the desert its monotonous look. Water, scarce as it is, is the dominant force working here. Flash floods carry great chunks of rock down to the canyon bottom. Water sculpts the cliffs and has carved the great "V" you're hiking in.

Coyote melons, bitter-tasting to people and to the coyotes as well, dot the wash. The melons dry in the sun and the gourds blow around the wash.

Before long, you'll come to a barrier across the wash preventing off-road vehicles from ascending into the upper reaches of the canyon. Past the barrier, the canyon widens and it's an easy 2-mile hike over soft sand back to Bow Willow Campground.

Water, not wind, has carved this canyon.

Carrizo Badlands

Canyon Sin Nombre Trail

Terrain: Slot canyon in awesomely eroded badlands.
Highlights: "A Walk Through Geologic Time."
Distance: 4 miles round-trip from mouth of canyon; 5½ miles round-trip from Highway S–2.
Degree of difficulty: Easy to moderate.

From the Carrizo Badlands Overlook, you can peer down at 10 miles of folded and twisted terrain. Although the badlands look impenetrable, there are ways into the maze of cliffs, caves, and winding washes. One such way into the badlands is via Canyon Sin Nombre, located below the overlook.

"Canyon Without a Name" is not the dark and scary place its name might suggest. Its rocky walls, sculpted into a variety of shapes and patterns, are a mosaic of blacks, browns, and grays.

The colorful canyon is a great walk; in fact, park interpreters refer to the badlands and the various geological ages represented there as "a walk through time." Layer upon layer of deposits from ancient lakes and seas have been tilted this way and that.

The sediments making up the badlands have been shaped and sculpted over many years by wind and the scant rainfall and, more profoundly, by rare flash floods. Only relatively recently in geologic time—within the last 20,000 years—has this land become a desert, say scientists.

Canyon Sin Nombre is open to four-wheel-drive travel, as are most of the larger washes and ravines in the Carrizo Badlands. The canyon is not a major route of travel, however. On most weekdays you can expect to meet more two-legged than four-wheeled visitors.

Directions to trailhead: Reach the Carrizo Badlands in the southern end of Anza-Borrego Desert State Park by exiting Interstate 8 onto Highway S–2. Drive 12 miles north to the Carrizo Badlands Overlook. Just north of the overlook at mileage marker 51.3 on the east side of the road is the signed turnoff for Canyon Sin Nombre. Park in the turnout just off the highway. High-clearance vehicles can proceed ¾-mile down the dirt road and park alongside the road about 200 yards from the entrance to the canyon. It's sandy, narrow, and rugged inside the canyon—strictly for four-wheel drive or walking.

The walk: Walk past some big barrel cactus into the mouth of the canyon. At the canyon entrance are brown and gray sedimentary layers estimated to be 1 to 3 million years old. In some places, once-horizontal sedimentary rocks are now vertical. Some canyon walls show S-shaped layers; the rock has been twisted downward, upward, and downward again.

The first 2 miles of Canyon Sin Nombre are the most interesting. Look for natural bridges and arches, rock formations that resemble castle walls, nests of ravens hidden on high. The jeep road eventually emerges at Carrizo Creek and links with other four-wheel-drive roads.

6. Imperial Valley

A diversity of landscapes, from sprawling farmland to a huge salt-water sea, from moonscape-looking mountains near the Mexican border to mammoth sand dunes near the Arizona border, make up the Imperial Valley. Agriculture is king in the southeastern portion of the Colorado Desert; some of the most productive farmland in the world is in the Imperial Valley. Nevertheless, the area has much to offer the hiker who knows when and where to step away from Highway 111.

Past the town of Coachella, Highway 111 becomes known as the North Shore Road and dips below sea level for much of its run to Brawley. The road is most interesting on an early winter morning when sunrise colors the Orocopia Mountains to the east and the Salton Sea to the west. Highlighting the scene are smoke trees, whose slate-gray branches from a distance resemble the plume made by a campfire.

Highway 111 edges close to the Salton Sea, one of the world's largest inland bodies of saltwater, often referred to in the 1930s as "Coachella Valley's Sea of Galilee." A thousand years ago an immense lake filled the desert basin. Then over a period of hundreds of years the desert heat reduced the sea to a vast expanse of gleaming white salt flats that remained until 1905, when the Colorado River overflowed its banks, flooded the Imperial Valley, and poured into the Salton Sink. When the flood was finally checked two years later, a lake had been formed. Evaporation reduced the Salton Sea to its present size (35 miles by 15 miles), which has nearly stabilized because of drainage from Imperial Valley irrigation.

Large campgrounds line the Salton Sea, the winter home of many a "snowbird"—long-term campers who've escaped colder climes for a season in the California desert. Bird-watching is simply spectacular at the Salton Sea National Wildlife Refuge. Snowbirds—and hikers—also enjoy the Algodones Dunes, handsome sand hills that reach 300 feet in height.

Salton Sea State Recreation Area

Ironwood Nature Trail

> **Terrain:** Salton Sea shoreline.
> **Highlights:** Abundant desert flora; swimming, beach.
> **Distance:** From the visitor center to Mecca Beach is 2 miles
>   round-trip; to Corvina Beach is 4½ miles round-trip.
> **Degree of difficulty:** Easy.

Between the desert and the Salton Sea is an intriguing, sun-baked shoreline quite unlike any other locale in the California desert. Some 18 miles of Salton Sea shoreline within the Salton Sea State Recreation Area invite the camper, angler, swimmer, and sunbather. Hikers will enjoy Ironwood Nature Trail, which explores the shoreline between the visitor center and Mecca Beach.

The 15-mile-wide, 35-mile-long Salton Sea was formed in 1905 when Colorado River floodwaters overwhelmed an Imperial Valley dike during construction of the All-American Canal. For two years water poured into the Salton Sink, an ancient seabed.

Surrounding rivers, washes, and canals continue to refill the lake with a combination of rainwater and agricultural runoff. Fertilizers and other minerals contribute to the high salinity (more than 10 percent "saltier" than the Pacific Ocean) of the Salton Sea.

You can learn more about the origins, present dilemmas, and possible ecological fate of the Salton Sea at the visitor center located near the park's harbor. Obtain a nature trail brochure and walk to the trailhead from here, or drive to campsite 32 in the headquarters campground known as Los Frijoles Camp.

Plan to catch some rays or take a swim at trail's end. Sandy Mecca Beach is a popular swimming area. Showers are available to wash off the film of salt and plankton that coats the swimmer.

Directions to trailhead: Salton Sea State Recreation Area is located 25 miles southeast of Indio on Highway 111.

The walk: From the campground, enjoy the 30-stop nature trail that explores everything from salt to salt cedars to smoke trees. When you reach Mecca Beach, you can either return the way you came or pick your own route closer to shore.

If you want to extend your hike, continue walking along the shoreline to undeveloped Corvina Beach Campground or as far as you choose.

Salton Sea National Wildlife Refuge

Rock Hill Trail

> **Terrain:** Marshlands, volcanic butte.
> **Highlights:** Great bird-watching.
> **Distance:** 2 miles round-trip.
> **Degree of difficulty:** Easy.

"Binoculars. Don't leave home without them," could be the motto of the Salton Sea Wildlife Refuge. In fact, few visitors who traipse the shores of the salty sea are found without their field glasses.

"We're in all the bird books," a ranger offers as explanation for why some 30,000 bird-watchers a year flock to this remote wildlife sanctuary.

Most noticeable of the feathered visitors and residents are the geese, particularly the loud-honking Canada geese who fly here in their distinctive V-shaped formation. Also easy to spot are the large snow geese and the Ross geese, white geese that are similar to, but smaller than, the snow geese.

In addition to the geese, bird-watchers spot several kinds of waterfowl—mergansers, wigeons, and teals. Endangered species include the Yuma clapper rail, the California brown pelican, the bald eagle, and the peregrine falcon. Other winged creatures seen at the refuge are bats and butterflies.

During the winters of 1992 and 1994, thousands of eared grebes died at the refuge. Scientists believe the birds were poisoned by a toxic form of algae blooming in the huge salty lake. The algae are likely nourished by fertilizers and other nitrogen-based pollutants, called nutrients, that flow into the Salton Sea from nearby farms, and perhaps even by sewage originating at Mexicali, Mexico. Aquatic biologists are studying the problem and trying to determine why the grebes were the only bird species affected by exposure to the algae.

Rock Hill Trail explores a kind of habitat that even the most experienced hikers may never have encountered: a coverstrip—trees and shrubs found along dikes that separate farm fields. Mesquite and paloverde in such coverstrips provide food and protection for wildlife. Characteristic coverstrip birds include Gambel's quail, mourning dove, and loggerhead shrike.

The refuge, which is open all year, is especially attractive in winter when the migratory birds are in residence. A tiny visitor center, an observation platform, and a shaded picnic area welcome bird-watchers.

Directions to trailhead: From Highway 111, 3½ miles north of Calipatria, turn west on Sinclair Road and proceed 6 miles to the Salton Sea National Wildlife Refuge headquarters and visitor center.

The walk: From the refuge's little observation platform, the path heads west along a dike for ½-mile. To the south is a geothermal energy plant that captures steam from deep within the earth to drive turbines and generate electricity.

The trail turns north as it reaches the Salton Sea shoreline, lined with birds and bird-watchers. A brief ascent brings the hiker to the top of Rock Hill, a small volcanic butte. Enjoy the bird's-eye view of the Salton Sea, then return the way you came.

Bird-watchers, anglers, and walkers enjoy the shores of the Salton Sea.

Algodones Dunes

Algodones Dunes Trail

Terrain: 200 to 300-foot-high sand hills.
Highlights: California's most extensive dune system, spring wildflowers.
Distance: 3 to 6 miles round-trip.
Degree of difficulty: Easy to moderate.
Precautions: No trail; difficult to navigate back from dunes.

In the mideastern Colorado Desert is a slice of the Middle East—miles of sand dunes that rise out of the desert floor like a mirage. California's largest mass of dunes, known variously as the Imperial Dunes, Sand Hills, Algodones National Natural Landmark, and Glamis Dunes, extends 45 miles northeast from the Mexican border along the eastern edge of the Imperial Valley.

Passage of the landmark California Desert Protection Act in October 1994 gave wilderness designation to some 22,000 acres of dunes formerly known as the Algodones Outstanding Natural Area. Off-highway vehicles will continue to be allowed to swarm over the southern two-thirds of the dune system, while nature lovers may walk in peace through the new wilderness.

Dune walking over the breathtakingly beautiful sandscape is a joy, particularly in spring when the foredunes are festooned with desert wildflowers.

The dunes emerged long ago when a series of lakes existed in the Salton Sea basin; when these Colorado River–fed lakes dried up during drought years, winds carried their shoreline and bottom sands southeastward and deposited them as dunes.

While constant movement of sand, summer temperatures reaching above 110°F, and annual rainfall of less than 2 inches are not environmental conditions that would seem to encourage life, a splendid diversity of plants and animals have adapted, indeed thrive, in the harsh dune ecosystem.

The ubiquitous creosote bushes on the edge of the dunes are accompanied by smaller, more unusual flora extending into the heart of the dunes: desert buckwheat, witchgrass, sandpaper plant, and the silver-leafed dune sunflower.

What little water reaches the dunes—the scant rainfall and some flash-flood runoff from the nearby Chocolate Mountains—gives rise to often stunning spring wildflower displays. Evening primrose, purple sand verbena, and orange mallow splash color on the sand.

Spring is also when the desert lilies bloom. Clusters of the large, white, funnel-shaped flowers adorn the tall (nearly 6 feet high) plants. Desert lilies can usually be found growing in large numbers on the north side of Highway 78, across the road from the Bureau of Land Management (BLM) ranger station.

Some unusual creatures call the dunes home. The banded gecko, a small lizard, has notched, interlocking eyelids that keep sand out of its eyes; if sand does manage to land on its eyeballs, its extremely long tongue can lick them clean. Geckos are mostly nocturnal and are thus rarely seen; however, they're sometimes heard. One of the few lizards with a voice, they can be heard calling on spring evenings—presumably for a mate.

The Couch's spadefoot toad, which uses its shovel-like hind feet to burrow in the sand, dwells on the east side of the dunes. These toads may hibernate 10 months, then emerge by the thousands after a rain to lay their eggs in shallow pools of water.

No trails cross the dunes. The best hiking is in the wilderness area north of Highway 78. Begin at the BLM ranger station and hike north into the dunes, or better yet, hike west into the dunes from Niland Road.

Two campgrounds are found near Highway 78, but they're "weekend cities" oriented to the needs of the thousands of motorized dune riders who arrive here in winter and spring. More mellow camping alternatives for the environmentally minded dune visitor are the BLM's Long Term Visitor areas located off Interstate 8 east of El Centro.

Directions to trailhead: From Interstate 10 in Indio, exit on Highway 111. Head southeast past the Salton Sea to Brawley. Drive east on Highway 78 some 20 miles to the western edge of the dunes and the BLM's Cahuilla Ranger Station and Visitor Information Center. You can park at the visitor center, cross Highway 78, and walk north into the dunes.

To really get away from it all, continue east on Highway 78 6 miles past the visitor center to the hamlet of Glamis. Turn left on unsigned Niland Road, a well-graded dirt road just west of the railroad tracks, and drive 5 or 6 miles. No developed parking exists; leave your vehicle in the sandy area between the road and the railroad tracks.

The walk: From Niland Road, you'll walk 1½ miles west to reach the main part of the dunes. Because few prominent landmarks (natural or built) exist in the area, pay attention to the route you take. It's easy navigating toward the prominent dunes, but much more difficult finding your way back to where you left your vehicle.

Mesquite Mine

Mesquite Mine Overlook Trail

Terrain: Cactus- and ocotillo-dotted slopes of Chocolate
  Mountains.
Highlights: Learn about California's second-largest gold mine.
Distance: 1 mile round-trip.
Degree of difficulty: Easy.

Nineteenth-century prospectors probed the Chocolate Mountains
and found "gold in them thar hills," but their discoveries were but a
fraction of the precious mineral hidden in the rock hereabouts.
Today the Mesquite Mine, California's second-largest, produces
more than 200,000 ounces of gold a year.

You can fantasize about owning a gold mine while walking the
Mesquite Mine Overlook Trail, a 14-stop interpreted path that ex-
plains the operation of a modern gold mine as well as the habits of
local flora and wildlife. Let's see . . . 200,000 ounces a year at $396
an ounce equals $79 million. Not bad diggings for Santa Fe Pacific
Gold Corporation, the mine's owner.

Fainthearted environmentalists should skip this trail, which pres-
sents the mining industry's view of the controversial practice of

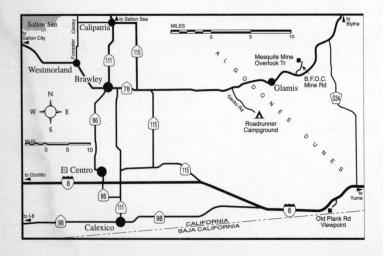

"heap leaching" (heaping ore in large mounds and washing it with a cyanide solution that leaches, or dissolves, the gold out).

If heap leaching and the fact that the mine moves around millions of tons of "waste rock" a year don't make a conservationist cringe, there's more: the mine operator supports a proposal to bring freight trains full of Southland garbage here to dump into the holes it's dug.

Directions to trailhead: From Highway 78, some 10 miles east of the Bureau of Land Management's Cahuilla Ranger Station and Visitor Information Center in the Algodones Dunes, turn north on well-signed, paved B.F.O.C. Mine Road. Proceed 3 miles to the signed trailhead and ample parking, just short of the entrance to the mine.

The walk: Mesquite Mine Overlook Trail, open daily from 8:00 A.M. to 4:00 P.M., climbs an ironwood- and paloverde-dotted slope for a view of the Chocolate Mountains to the north, the Algodones Dunes to the west, the vast surrounding desert, and of course the huge Mesquite Mine just below.

Valley of the Moon

Valley of the Moon Trail

> **Terrain:** Boulder-strewn Jacumba Mountains on California–Mexico border.
> **Highlights:** View of two countries; surreal Valley of the Moon.
> **Distance:** To Valley of the Moon is 6 miles round-trip with 700-foot elevation gain.
> **Degree of difficulty:** Moderate.

From the jumbled rock formations at the border are views of two countries (Mexico and the United States), two counties (Imperial and San Diego), and two mountain ranges (the Jacumba Mountains and the Sierra Juarez).

The granite outcroppings resemble those of Joshua Tree National Park, though the surrounding Jacumba Mountains are sprinkled with pinyon pine, not Joshuas. On the U.S. side of the border the mountains are known as the Jacumba range, but more internationally minded geographers consider them to be an extension of Baja's 100-mile-long Sierra Juarez.

Trails in the Jacumbas lead very close to the border. The range's high point, 4,548-foot Blue Angels Peak, is crowned with an international boundary marker, a 10-foot-high steel obelisk. A more unsavory indication of border activity is Smugglers Cave, supposedly where bandits circa 1875 laid low; local lore also has it that the cave figured in the smuggling of opium and Chinese laborers.

The most intriguing sight to see is a surreal landscape known as Valley of the Moon. Sunset photography around here is superb.

Until the Jacumbas received a wilderness designation, several four-wheel-drive roads led into the range. Now the cracked stacks of granite, the caves, and the narrow passageways can be reached only by foot.

A second hike that you might consider begins at the saddle on the way to Valley of the Moon. From the saddle you can follow jeep roads and then make a short cross-country climb to the top of Blue Angels Peak. The pinyon pine–spiked summit offers good views of the border country. Hold onto your hat—it's often mighty windy on top. Round-trip distance from the trailhead is 5 miles with a 1,300-foot elevation gain.

Directions to trailhead: From Interstate 8, some 90 miles east of San Diego and just west of the Imperial County line, exit on In-Ko-Pah Peak Road. Head southwest along the frontage road for ¼-mile, then turn left onto an unsigned dirt road. Drive ¾-mile up the road to a parking area.

The walk: Hike up the jeep road to a saddle. A spur road forks left to Smugglers Cave, defaced by graffiti.

From the saddle, veer right at the first junction, left at the second. As the road descends, you'll ignore minor spurs that lead to primitive camps. The road climbs a bit toward minor, but prominent, Tahe Peak. Stick to the main road, keeping left and avoiding the spur road that leads to an abandoned amethyst mine.

After winding east, then south around the base of Tahe Peak, you'll turn east once more and descend into Valley of the Moon.

Explore the lunar landscape by following a couple of jeep roads or by navigating among the big boulders. Stay oriented to the road; it's easy to lose your bearings in this strange terrain.

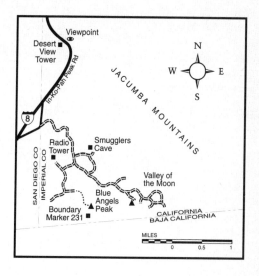

The beauty of Palm Springs has attracted nature lovers and health- and pleasure-seekers for more than a century.

7. Palm Springs and the Coachella Valley

Early in the 20th century, it was called a Desert Eden, Our Araby, and a Garden in the Sun. Now it's called a Desert Hollywood, Fairway Living, and Rodeo Drive East.

Palm Springs today means different things to different people, but one thing is for certain—the golf courses, condos, and country clubs of the resort are a far cry from what the first residents of Agua Caliente intended.

What most Palm Springs pioneers intended was to leave this desert land more or less alone. Turn-of-the-century health seekers and nature lovers recognized their discovery for what it was—a true oasis. Here was a palm-dotted retreat where an ancient hot springs gushed forth. Here was nature simple and unadorned.

Some residents championed the creation of Palm Canyon National Monument to preserve the canyons on the outskirts of Palm Springs known collectively as the Indian Canyons—Palm, Murray, and Andreas. The national monument was approved by Congress in 1922, but no funds were allocated and the palm canyons never did win National Park Service protection.

Finally, however, in 1990, a sizable portion of the palm canyons, as well as the surrounding mountains, came under federal protection with the establishment of the Santa Rosa Mountains National Scenic Area, administered by the Bureau of Land Management.

Fortunately for the modern visitor, there yet remains a wild side of Palm Springs—parks, preserves, and special places that offer opportunities to see the desert of old. Palm Springs wildlife, not to be confused with the Palm Springs wild life enjoyed by thousands of college students who come here during spring break, can be viewed in a number of quiet and picturesque locales, both near town and in the surrounding Coachella Valley.

"Essentially, the desert is Nature in her simplest expression," wrote nature writer and Palm Springs resident Joseph Smeaton Chase. The Living Desert, Palm Canyon, Big Morongo Canyon, and the Coachella Valley Preserve are places for the hiker to commune with this simple nature.

Big Morongo Canyon

Big Morongo Canyon Trail

> **Terrain:** Year-round creek, thickets of willow and cotton-wood.
> **Highlights:** Lush canyon, abundant bird life.
> **Distance:** To waterfall is 2½ miles round-trip; to canyon mouth is 12 miles round-trip with 1,900-foot elevation gain.
> **Degree of difficulty:** Easy to moderately strenuous.

Two deserts—the Mojave and the Colorado—meet at Big Morongo Canyon, tucked in the Little San Bernardino Mountains on the San Bernardino–Riverside county line. Big Morongo Canyon Reserve bridges these two desert worlds and offers the hiker a chance to explore one of the state's largest natural oases.

For many centuries native peoples used Big Morongo Canyon as a passageway between the high and low deserts. The last of these nomads to inhabit the canyon were a group of Serrano Indians known as the Morongo, for whom the canyon is named. When white settlers entered the area in the mid-19th century, the Morongos were forced onto a reservation and the canyon became the property of ranchers. Today, Big Morongo Canyon is managed and protected by the Nature Conservancy and the U.S. Bureau of Land Management.

The relative abundance of water is the key to both Big Morongo's long history of human occupation and its botanical uniqueness. Several springs bubble up in the reserve, and one of the California desert's very few year-round creeks flows through the canyon. Dense thickets of cottonwood and willow, as well as numerous water-loving shrubs, line Big Morongo Creek. This lush, crowded riparian vegetation contrasts sharply with the well-spaced creosote community typical of the high and dry slopes of the reserve and of the open desert beyond.

The oasis at Big Morongo is a crucial water supply for the fox, bobcat, raccoon, coyote, and bighorn sheep. Gopher snakes, rosy boas, chuckwallas, and California tree frogs are among the amphibians and reptiles in residence. The permanent water supply also makes it possible for the showy Western tiger swallowtail and other butterflies to thrive, along with several species of dragonflies and water bugs.

Big Morongo Canyon is best known for its wide variety of birds, which are numerous because the canyon is not only at the intersection of two deserts, but also at the merging of two climate zones— arid and coastal. These climates, coupled with the wet world of the oasis, make the preserve an attractive stopover for birds on their spring and fall migrations.

More than 200 bird species have been sighted, including the rare vermilion flycatcher and the least Bell's vireo. Commonly seen all-year residents include starlings, house finches, and varieties of quail and hummingbirds.

For the hiker, the preserve offers several short loop trails ranging from ¼-mile to a mile long. Some of the wetter canyon-bottom sections of trail are crossed by wooden boardwalks, which keep hikers dry and fragile creekside flora from being trampled. Desert Wash, Cottonwood, Willow, Yucca Ridge, and Mesquite trails explore the environments suggested by their names.

A longer path, Canyon Trail, travels the 6-mile length of Big Morongo Canyon. You could make this a one-way, all-downhill journey by arranging a car shuttle or by having someone pick you up on Indian Avenue. Families with small children or the leg-weary will enjoy a 2½-mile round-trip canyon walk to a small waterfall.

Directions to trailhead: From Interstate 10, 15 miles east of Banning and a bit past the Highway 111 turnoff to Palm Springs,

exit on Highway 62. Drive 10 miles north to the signed turnoff on your right for Big Morongo Wildlife Preserve. Turn east and after 1/10-mile you'll see the preserve's service road leading to a parking area.

To reach the end of the trail at the mouth of Big Morongo Canyon, you'll take the Indian Avenue exit from Highway 62 and drive exactly a mile to a dirt road on your left. A DIP sign precedes the turnoff, and a pump enclosed by a chain-link fence suggests your parking space.

The walk: From the parking lot at Big Morongo Wildlife Preserve, you may pick up the trail by the interpretive displays or join the dirt road that leads past the caretaker's residence. Pick up a copy of the *Big Morongo Bird List* from a roadside dispenser.

Off to the right of the old ranch road, you'll see a cottonwood-lined pasture and a barn built in the 1880s. Often the road is muddy, so detour with the signed and aptly named Mesquite Trail, which utilizes a wooden boardwalk to get over the wet spots. As you stand on the boardwalk above Big Morongo Creek, take a moment to listen to the sound of running water, the many chirping birds, and the croaking frogs.

Canyon Trail meanders with the creek for a gentle mile or so before arriving at a corrugated metal check dam that has created a small waterfall. For the less energetic, this is a good turnaround point.

The trail continues descending through the canyon with Big Morongo Creek until, a bit over 3 miles from the trailhead, the creek suddenly disappears. Actually, the water continues flowing underground through layers of sand.

The canyon widens and so does the trail. About 5 miles from the trailhead is the south gate of the preserve. The canyon mouth and every inanimate object in the vicinity have been shot to hell by off-the-mark marksmen. Compensating for Big Morongo's somewhat inglorious end is a stirring view of snowcapped Mount San Jacinto, which lies straight ahead. Stick to your right at every opportunity as you leave the canyon and a dirt road will soon deliver you to Indian Avenue.

Thousand Palms Oasis, Coachella Valley Preserve

McCallum, Smoke Tree Ranch, Indian Palms Trails

Terrain: Second-largest palm oasis.
Highlights: Wild side of Coachella Valley; intriguing plants and reptiles.
Distance: 1- to 5-mile loop.
Degree of difficulty: Easy to moderate.

If it looks like a movie set, don't be surprised.

Thousand Palms Oasis was the setting for Cecil B. DeMille's 1924 silent film epic, *King of Kings,* and the 1969 movie *Tell Them Willie Boy Is Here* starring Robert Redford, Robert Blake, and Katharine Ross. The oasis is something special, and deserving of protection, but that's not why Coachella Valley Preserve was established. The reserve's raison d'être is habitat for the threatened Coachella Valley fringe-toed lizard.

For the most part, *Uma inornata* goes about the business of being a lizard beneath the surface of sand dunes, but scientists have been able to discover some of the peculiar habits of this creature, which manages to survive in places where a summer's day surface temperature may reach 160°F.

The 8-inch reptile is also known as the "sand swimmer" for its ability to dive through sand dunes. Its entrenching tool–shaped skull rams through the sand, while round scales on its skin reduce friction as it "swims." Fringes (large scales) on its toes give the lizard traction—as well as its name.

Alas, all is not fun in the sun for the fringe-toed lizard. The creature must avoid becoming dinner for such predators as roadrunners, snakes, and loggerhead shrikes. But the biggest threat to the lizard has been real estate development and consequent loss of habitat.

Fortunately for the fringe-toed lizard, real estate developers, the U.S. Bureau of Land Management, Congress, the California Department of Fish and Game, the U.S. Wildlife Service, and the Nature Conservancy were able to find a common ground and establish a 13,000-acre preserve in 1986. Some conservationists believe the

$25 million price tag may be the most expensive single species preservation effort of all time.

Still, the reserve would be something special even without its namesake lizard. It protects flora and fauna once common in the Coachella Valley before it grew grapefruit, golf courses, and subdivisions.

Thousand Palms Oasis is California's second-largest collection of native California fan palms. Thousand Palms, along with Indian Palms, Horseshoe Palms, and a couple of other oases in the reserve, came into existence as the result of earthquake faults that brought water to the surface.

Before the reserve was set aside, the Thousand Palms area was purchased by turn-of-the-century rancher Louis Wilhelm and his family. The Wilhelms built "Palm House" (now the reserve's visitor center) and by the 1930s were using it as a commissary for campers, scientists, Scout troops, and anyone else who wanted to enjoy a weekend in one of their palm-shaded cottages.

Hikers can explore Coachella Valley Preserve on a half-dozen trails. Three of these trails depart from Thousand Palms Oasis. The shortest, a 15-minute walk, is *Smoke Tree Ranch Trail,* which encircles the palms oasis. There is good bird-watching in the mesquite thickets and among the smoke trees. Watch for the smoke trees' bright blue and purple flowers in May or June.

Don't miss *McCallum Trail* (1½ miles round-trip), a nature trail that meanders by a jungle of willows, palms, cottonwoods, and mes-

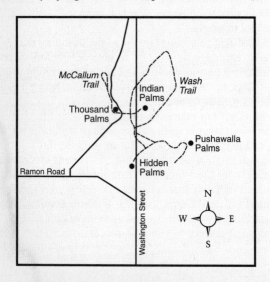

quite. At the trailhead, pick up an interpretive pamphlet that's keyed to numbered posts along the path.

Indian Palms Trail leads ½-mile to small Indian Palms Oasis.

More ambitious hikers will head for *Wash Trail,* which, true to its name, winds through washes in the northern portion of the reserve. You can also visit Bee Rock Mesa, where Malpais Indians camped 5,000 years ago, hike into adjoining Indio Hills County Park, and visit more oases—Horseshoe Palms and Pushawalla Palms.

Directions to trailhead: From Interstate 10, about 10 miles east of where Highway 111 leads off to Palm Springs, exit on Washington Street/Ramon Road. Head north on Washington Street, which bends west and continues as Ramon Road. Soon after the bend, turn right (north again) onto Thousand Palms Canyon Road. Continue to the entrance to Coachella Valley Preserve and park in the dirt lot.

Pick your way through the palms for a delightful desert walk.

Palm Springs Desert Museum

Museum and Lykken Trails

Terrain: Steep western base of Mount San Jacinto above the city.

Highlights: Palm Spring vistas.

Distance: From Palm Springs Desert Museum to Desert Riders Overlook is 2 miles round-trip with 800-foot elevation gain; to Ramon Road is 4 miles round-trip with 800-foot gain.

Degree of difficulty: Moderate.

Palm Springs today is a curious sight—a chain of sparkling green islands on the desert sand. For a good overview of the resort, hikers can join Museum and Lykken trails.

This hike in the hills begins at Palm Springs Desert Museum, where natural science exhibits recreate the unique ecology of Palm Springs and the surrounding Colorado Desert. Displays interpret the astonishing variety of plant and animal life as well as the powerful geological forces that shaped the land. The museum also has exhibits portraying the original inhabitants of the Coachella Valley.

Steep Museum Trail ascends the western base of Mount San Jacinto. Letters painted on the rocks suggest that Museum was once a nature trail. After a mile's climb, Museum Trail reaches a junction with Lykken Trail. This trail, formerly known as Skyline Trail, winds through the Palm Springs hills north to Tramway Road and south to Ramon Road.

Skyline Trail was renamed Lykken Trail in 1972 in honor of Carl Lykken, a Palm Springs pioneer and the town's first postmaster. Lykken, who arrived in 1913, owned a general merchandise store, and later a department and hardware store. Early Palm Springs social life consisted of stopping at the Desert Inn to check if any new and interesting guests had arrived, then dropping by Carl Lykken's store to pick up the mail, make a phone call (Lykken had the first telephone), and catch up on all the gossip.

Directions to trailhead: From Highway 111 (Palm Canyon Drive) in the middle of downtown Palm Springs, turn west on Tahquitz Way, then make a right on Museum Drive. Park in Palm Springs Desert Museum's north lot.

The trail begins back of the museum, between the museum and an administration building, next to a plaque honoring Carl Lykken. The trail is closed during the summer months for health reasons (yours).

The walk: The trail ascends the rocky slope above the museum. Soon you'll intersect a private road, jog left, then resume trail walking up the mountainside. As you rapidly gain elevation, the view widens from the Desert Fashion Plaza to the outskirts of Palm Springs to the wide-open spaces of the Coachella Valley.

A mile's ascent brings you to a picnic area, built by the Desert Riders, local equestrians whose membership included Carl Lykken. One Desert Rider, former Palm Springs Mayor Frank Bogart, is a dedicated trail enthusiast whose efforts have contributed much to the state's trail system.

Bear left (south) on Lykken Trail, which travels the hills above town before descending to Ramon Road near the mouth of Tahquitz Canyon. You can follow Ramon Road to downtown Palm Springs or return the way you came.

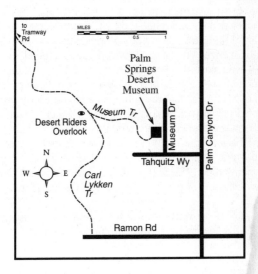

The Living Desert

Jaeger Nature Trail

Terrain: Botanic garden, brittlebush-dotted floodplain.
Highlights: Great introduction to desert plant and wildlife.
Distance: 2-mile loop through Living Desert Reserve; return
   via Eisenhower Trail, Eisenhower Mountain is 5 miles
   round-trip with 500-foot elevation gain.
Degree of difficulty: Easy to moderate.

A superb introduction to desert plant and animal life, the Living
Desert is a combination zoo, botanic garden, and hiking area. The
1,200-acre nonprofit facility is dedicated to conservation, educa-
tion, and research.

Gardens represent major desert regions, including California's
Mojave, Arizona's Sonoran, and Mexico's Chihuahuan. Wildlife-
watchers will enjoy observing coyotes in their burrows and bighorn
sheep atop their mountain peak. The reserve also has a walk-
through aviary and a pond inhabited by the rare desert pupfish.

Nature and hiking trails provide an opportunity to form an even
closer acquaintance with an uncrowded, undeveloped sandscape.
Easy trails lead past the Arabian oryx and bighorn sheep, past
desert flora with name tags and ecosystems with interpretive displays, and over to areas that resemble the open desert of yesteryear.

Presidents Eisenhower, Nixon, Ford, and Reagan relaxed in Palm
Springs. Eisenhower spent many winters at the El Dorado Country
Club at the base of the mountain that now bears his name. Palm
Desert boosters petitioned the Federal Board of Geographic
Names to name the 1,952-foot peak (coincidentally, 1952 was the
year of his election) for part-time Palm Springs resident Dwight D.
Eisenhower.

The first part of the walk through the Living Desert uses a nature
trail named after the great naturalist Edmund Jaeger. It's keyed to a
booklet available at the entrance station. An inner loop of ⅔-mile and
an outer loop of 1½ miles lead past a wide array of desert flora and 60
interpretive stops. A longer loop can be made using Canyon Trail and
Eisenhower Trail. The hike to Ike's peak ascends about halfway up
the bald mountain and offers great views of the Coachella Valley.

Directions to trailhead: From Highway 111 in Palm Desert, turn south on Portola Avenue and drive 1½ miles south to the park. Hours: 9:00 A.M.–5:00 P.M.; closed mid-June to the end of August.

The walk: The trail begins at the exhibit buildings. Follow either the numbered nature trail, beginning at number one, or make a short rightward detour to the bighorn sheep enclosure. The trail junctions once more and you begin heading up the alluvial plain of Deep Canyon. Walking up the wash, you'll observe the many moisture-loving plants that thrive in such environments, including smoke trees, desert willows, and paloverde.

Stay right at the next junction and begin the outer loop of the Jaeger Nature Trail. You'll pass plenty of that common desert dweller, the creosote bush, and wind along the base of some sand dunes.

The trail climbs out of the wash and onto a kind of plain that true desert rats call a *bajada*. Here you'll find a quail guzzler, which stores rainwater to aid California's state bird in the hot summer months. And here you'll find a junction with Canyon Trail (the south loop of the Eisenhower Trail).

Canyon Trail heads up the *bajada*. After climbing through a little canyon, the path winds up the south slope of Eisenhower Mountain to a picnic area and a plaque describing the region's date industry.

From the picnic area, you'll descend Eisenhower Mountain, getting good views of the mountains and the Coachella Valley. After passing the signed Eisenhower trailhead, you'll reach the north loop of the Jaeger Nature Trail and begin heading west down the brittlebush-dotted floodplain back to the exhibit buildings and the central part of the reserve.

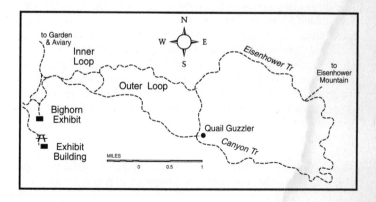

Murray and Andreas Canyons

Murray Canyon Trail

> **Terrain:** Two palm-lined canyons.
> **Highlights:** Hundreds of palms, lush undergrowth.
> **Distance:** From Andreas Canyon to Murray Canyon is 2 miles round-trip with 200-foot elevation gain.
> **Degree of difficulty:** Easy.

In the foothills above Palm Springs are two lovely palm-lined canyons—Andreas and Murray. Both have hundreds of palms, crystalline streams, and dramatic rock walls. Andreas, with about 700 native California fan palms, and Murray, with about 1,000 palms, are among the most populous palm groves in the state. Both canyons are tributaries of nearby Palm Canyon, undisputed king of California's palm oases.

Both canyons honor Palm Springs pioneers. Andreas is named after a Cahuilla Indian chieftain of the late-19th century, while Murray honors irascible Scotsman and dedicated botanist Dr. Welwood Murray, who built a hotel/health resort in the very early days of Palm Springs. Many of those making their way to the Murray Hotel came for the curative climate and the rejuvenation of their health, but a number of literary figures also visited and these scribes soon spread the word that Palm Springs was a very special place indeed.

Andreas Canyon was once a summer retreat for the Agua Caliente band of the Cahuilla. The Indians spent the winter months in the warm Coachella Valley, then sought the relative coolness of Andreas and other palm canyons during the warmer months.

Unlike most palm oases, which are fed by underground springs or sluggish seeps, Andreas is watered by a running stream. Fortunately for the palms and other canyon life, white settlers were legally prevented from diverting this stream to the emerging village of Palm Springs. Ranchers and townspeople had to turn to the larger, but notoriously undependable, Whitewater River.

Meandering through the tall Washingtonias, hikers can travel some distance upstream through Andreas Canyon. Adding to the lush scene are alders and willows, cottonwoods and sycamores.

The trail between Andreas Canyon and Murray Canyon is only a mile long, but you can travel a few more miles up the canyons themselves.

Directions to trailhead: From the junction of Highway 111 and South Palm Canyon Drive in Palm Springs, proceed south on the latter road for 1½ miles, bearing right at a signed fork. After another mile you'll reach the Agua Caliente Indian Reservation tollgate.

Just after the tollgate, bear right at a signed fork and travel ¾-mile to Andreas Canyon picnic ground. The trail begins at the east end of this splendid picnic area. A sign suggests that Murray Canyon is 20 minutes away.

The walk: Notice the soaring, reddish brown rocks near the trailhead. At the base of these rocks are grinding holes once used by the Cahuilla.

The trail runs south along the base of the mountains. A dramatic backdrop to the path is the desert-facing side of the San Jacinto Mountains.

It's an easy walk, occasionally following a dry streambed. Here, away from water, you encounter more typical desert flora: cholla, hedgehog cacti, burrobush.

When you reach Murray Canyon, you can follow the palms and stream quite a distance up-canyon. Joining the palms are willows, cottonwoods, mesquite, arrowweed, and desert lavender. Mistletoe is sometimes draped atop the mesquite and attracts lots of birds.

As you take the trail back to Andreas Canyon, you can't help noticing the luxury housing and resort life reaching toward the palm canyons. And you can't help being thankful that these tranquil palm oases are still ours to enjoy.

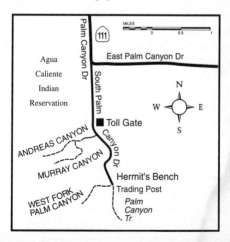

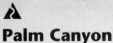

Palm Canyon

Palm Canyon Trail

> **Terrain:** Junglelike palm-filled oasis.
> **Highlights:** Greatest concentration of native palms in the United States.
> **Distance:** From Hermit's Bench to turnaround is 4 miles round-trip with 200-foot elevation gain.
> **Degree of difficulty:** Easy.

During the last few years much has been written in newspapers and magazine articles about Palm Canyon. Briefly stated, its charm consists in the startling combination of rocky gorges and canyons, essentially savage and desert-like, with the arboreal grace of tall, tropic-seeming palms growing in native loveliness beside a snow-few, gushing stream. If the effect of the whole were to be summed up in one word, I think the word would be, not grandeur, nor even beauty, but strangeness to a notable degree.

Joseph Smeaton Chase, 1922

Our Araby: Palm Springs and the Garden of the Sun

Long-forgotten trail rider and nature writer Joseph Smeaton Chase lived the last few years of his life in Palm Springs. He championed the creation of Palm Canyon National Monument in order to preserve the canyons located on the outskirts of Palm Springs, known collectively as the Indian Canyons—Palm, Murray, and Andreas.

The palm canyons never did achieve National Park Service protection, but they were spared from development and are now under the jurisdiction of the Agua Caliente Indians and the U.S. Bureau of Land Management's Santa Rosa Mountains National Scenic Area.

The hills and canyons bordering Palm Springs have the greatest concentration of palm trees in the United States, and in number of trees, Palm Canyon is the uncrowned king of America's desert oases. A meandering stream and lush undergrowth complement over 3,000 palms, creating a junglelike atmosphere in some places.

Palm fans will enjoy viewing the largest concentration of California fan palms while visiting the Agua Caliente Indian Reservation.

Directions to trailhead: From Interstate 10, exit on Highway 111 (Palm Canyon Drive) and proceed to downtown Palm Springs. Continue through town on Palm Canyon Drive. At a fork, Highway 111 veers east and becomes known as East Palm Canyon Drive. You head straight ahead, on South Palm Canyon Drive, following the signs to "Indian Canyons." You reach the Agua Caliente Indian tollgate, where you must pay a fee to enter tribal lands. The reservation is open daily from 8:30 A.M. to 5:00 P.M. Parking is a short distance beyond the tollgate at Hermit's Bench, where there is a trading post and a good view north into Palm Springs. Many signs remind visitors that they must be off the reservation before 5 P.M.

The walk: From the trading post, the trail descends into the canyon. Some of the palms stand 60 feet tall, with 3-foot trunk diameters. The trail follows the canyon for 2 miles to a tiny grotto that seems an ideal place to turn around.

Hearty adventurers will relish the challenge of proceeding up Palm Canyon 7 more miles, gaining 3,000 feet in elevation before reaching a junction with Highway 74, the Pines-to-Palms Highway. Note: This extremely strenuous hike is best done by beginning at the Highway 74 trailhead, hiking down Palm Canyon, and convincing a friend to pick you up at Hermit's Bench. Contact the Bureau of Land Management in Palm Springs for the latest trail advice.

Santa Rosa Wilderness

Cactus Spring Trail

Terrain: Mixture of high- and low-desert environments.
Highlights: Diverse flora, cottonwood-shaded creek.
Distance: From Pinyon Flat to Horsethief Creek is 5 miles round-trip with 900-foot elevation loss; to Cactus Spring is 9 miles round-trip with 300-foot elevation gain.
Degree of difficulty: Moderate to moderately strenuous.

The Santa Rosas are primarily a desert range and a unique blend of high- and low-desert environments. The desert-facing slopes of these mountains are treeless, as scorched and sparse as the desert itself. Throughout the foothills and canyons, lower Sonoran vegetation—chamise, barrel cactus, ocotillo, and waxy creosote—predominates. In some of the canyons with water on or near the surface, oases of native California fan palms form verdant islands on the sand. With an increase in elevation, the wrinkled canyons and dry arroyos give way to mountain crests bristling with pine and juniper.

The Santa Rosa Wilderness, set aside in 1984, lies within the boundaries of the San Bernardino National Forest. Another part of the Santa Rosa Mountains is under state stewardship; it provides protected habitat for the bighorn sheep. A third section, the Santa Rosa Mountains National Scenic Area, under U.S. Bureau of Land Management administration, was established in 1990.

When visiting the Santa Rosas, early California botanist and travel writer Charles Francis Saunders was so overwhelmed by the contrast between the harshness of the lower desert slopes and the relative gentleness of the higher slopes that he called it "a botanic version of the millennial day when lion and lamb shall lie down together." Saunders may have massacred a metaphor, but the hiker who dodges cholla and yucca, then takes a snooze upon a soft bed of pinyon pine needles, will find it easy to tell lion from lamb, botanically speaking.

Trails are few in the Santa Rosas; most are faint traces of Cahuilla Indian paths. The ancients climbed the mountains to hunt deer, gather pinyon pine nuts, and escape the desert heat. When the snows began, they descended from the high country to gentler wintering areas below.

Cactus Spring Trail, an old Indian path overhauled by the Forest Service, gives the hiker a wonderful introduction to the delights of the Santa Rosas. The trail first takes you to Horsethief Creek, a perennial waterway that traverses high-desert country. A hundred years ago, horse thieves pastured their stolen animals in this region before driving them to San Bernardino to sell. The cottonwood-shaded creek invites a picnic. Continuing on the trail, you'll arrive at Cactus Spring. Along the way is some wild country, as undisturbed as it was in 1774 when early Spanish trailblazer Juan Bautista de Anza first saw it.

Directions to trailhead: From Highway 111 in Palm Desert, drive 16 miles up Highway 74 to the Pinyon Flat Campground. (From Hemet, it's a 40-mile drive along Highway 74 to Pinyon Flat Campground.) Opposite the campground is Pinyon Flat Transfer Station Road, also signed "Elks Mountain Retreat." You'll follow this road about ¾-mile. Just before you reach the (trash) Transfer Station, a rough dirt road veers to the left. Follow this road 200 yards to its end.

The walk: Follow the dirt road east a short distance to Fire Road 7S01, then head south for ¼-mile. You'll then take the first road on your left. A sign reassures you that you are indeed on the way to Cactus Spring, and you'll soon pass the abandoned Dolomite Mine, where limestone was once quarried. Approximately ¼-mile past the mine site, the dirt road peters out and the trail begins. Here you'll find a sign and a trail register.

The trail bears to the east and dips in and out of several (usually) dry gullies. A ½-mile past the sign-in register, a sign welcomes you to the Santa Rosa Wilderness. Cactus Spring Trail does not contour over the hills, but zigs and zags, apparently without rhyme or reason. The bewitching, but easy-to-follow trail finally drops down to Horsethief Creek. At the creek crossing, Horsethief Camp welcomes the weary with flowing water and shade.

Return the same way, explore up and down the handsome canyon cut by Horsethief Creek, or continue to Cactus Spring.

To reach Cactus Spring, cross the creek, then climb east out of the canyon on a rough and steep trail past sentinel yuccas guarding the dry slopes. The trail stays with a wash for a spell (the route through the wash is unmarked except for occasional rock ducts), then gently ascends over pinyon pine–covered slopes. It's rolling, wild country, a good place to hide out. Alas, Cactus Spring, a few hundred yards north of the trail, is almost always dry.

Scorching sands and snowcapped peaks—the diversity of the desert.

Mount San Jacinto State Park

Desert View Trail

> **Terrain:** Diverse, palms-to-pines slopes of Mount San Jacinto.
> **Highlights:** Great desert vistas from cool mountaintop.
> **Distance:** From Mountain Station to Desert View is 2 miles round-trip; to Round Valley is 6 miles round-trip.
> **Degree of difficulty:** Easy to moderate.

Palm Springs Aerial Tramway makes it easy for hikers to enter Mount San Jacinto State Wilderness. Starting in Chino Canyon near Palm Springs, a tram takes passengers from 2,643-foot Lower Tramway Terminal (Valley Station) to 8,516-foot Upper Tramway Terminal (Mountain Station) at the edge of the wilderness.

The Swiss-made gondola rapidly leaves terra firma behind. Too rapidly, you think. It carries you over one of the most abrupt mountain faces in the world, over cliffs only a bighorn sheep can scale, over several life zones, from palms to pines. The view is fantastic.

Conservationists opposed construction of the tramway, pointing out that Mount San Jacinto's slopes were totally unsuited to the project's stated purpose—skiing. First proposed in the 1930s, the project was finally completed in 1963 after approval and funding by the State of California.

Now, most nature lovers enjoy witnessing, in just minutes, flora and fauna changes equivalent to those viewed on a motor trip from the Mojave Desert to the Arctic Circle. In pre-Tramway days, John Muir called the view "the most sublime spectacle to be found anywhere on this earth!"

For an introduction to the alpine environment of Mount San Jacinto State Park, take the short nature trail that begins at Mountain Station, then join Desert View Trail for a superb panorama of Palm Springs. After enjoying the view of the arid lands below, you can extend your hike by looping through lush Round Valley.

Directions to trailhead: From Highway 111 at the northern outskirts of Palm Springs, turn southwest on Tramway Road and drive 3½ miles to the tramway terminal.

The walk: From Mountain Station, walk down the paved pathway to the signed beginning of the trail to Desert View. You join the nature trail for a short distance, cross the path used by the "mule ride," and soon get the first of a couple of great desert views. The view takes in Palm Springs, Tahquitz, and other palm-lined canyons of the Agua Caliente Indian Reservation, along with the basin and hills of the Coachella Valley.

Continue on Desert View Trail, which makes a full circle and intersects with the path back up to Mountain Station. For a longer hike, walk through the Long Valley Picnic Area to the state park ranger station. Obtain a wilderness permit here.

Continue west on the trail, following the signs to Round Valley. The trail parallels Long Valley Creek through a mixed forest of pine and white fir, then climbs into lodgepole pine country. Lupine, monkey flower, scarlet bugler, and Indian paintbrush are some of the wildflowers that add seasonal splashes of color.

After you pass a junction with a trail leading toward Willow Creek, another ³⁄₁₀-mile of hiking brings you to Round Valley. There's a trail camp and a backcountry ranger station in the valley, and splendid places to picnic in the meadow or among the lodgepole pines. The truly intrepid hiker will head for the summit of Mount San Jacinto, a 3½-mile ascent from Round Valley.

An alternative to returning the same way is to retrace your steps ³⁄₁₀-mile to the junction with Willow Creek Trail, take this trail a mile through the pines to another signed junction, and follow the signed trail north back to Long Valley Ranger Station. This alternative adds only about ¼-mile to your day hike and allows you to make a loop.

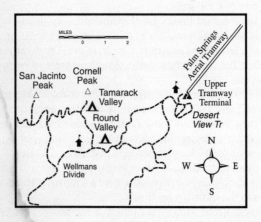

![Desert Divide logo icon]

Desert Divide

Spitler Peak Trail

> **Terrain:** Ridge on mountain-desert border.
> **Highlights:** Forest and desert vistas.
> **Distance:** From Apple Canyon to Desert Divide is 10 miles
> round-trip with 2,000-foot elevation gain; to Apache Peak
> is 12 miles round-trip with 2,600-foot gain; to Antsell Rock
> is 14 miles round-trip with 2,600-foot gain.
> **Degree of difficulty:** Strenuous.

Riding the Palm Springs Aerial Tramway and driving the Pines-to-Palms Highway are two ways to view the astonishing change in vegetation that occurs with a change in elevation in the San Jacinto Mountains. A third way to observe the startling contrast between desert and alpine environments is to hike up the backside of the San Jacinto Mountains to aptly named Desert Divide. The imposing granite divide, which reminds some mountaineers of the High Sierra, offers far-reaching views of the canyons back of Palm Springs and of the Coachella Valley.

Most visitors to the San Jacinto Mountains begin their explorations in Idyllwild or from the top of the tramway. Few hike—or even think about—Desert Divide. That's too bad, because this land of pine forest, wide meadows, and soaring granite peaks has much to offer.

The trail begins in Garner Valley, a long meadowland bordered by tall pines. Meandering across the valley floor is the South Fork of the San Jacinto River, whose waters are impounded at the lower end of the valley by Lake Hemet. Autumn brings a showy "river" of rust-colored buckwheat winding through the valley.

Spitler Peak Trail offers a moderate-to-strenuous route up to Desert Divide. You can enjoy the great views from the divide and call it a day right there, or you can join Pacific Crest Trail and continue to the top of Apache Peak or Antsell Rock.

Directions to trailhead: The hamlet of Mountain Center is some 20 miles up Highway 74 from Hemet and a few miles up Highway 243 from Idyllwild. From the intersection of Highway 243 (Banning-Idyllwild Highway) and Highway 74 in Mountain Center, proceed southeast on the latter highway. After 3 miles, turn left at the signed junction for Hurkey Creek County Park. Instead of turning into the park, you'll continue 1¾ miles on Apple Canyon Road to signed Spitler Peak Trail on the right. Park in the turnout just south of the trailhead.

The walk: Spitler Peak Trail begins among oak woodland and chaparral. The mellow, well-graded path contours quite some distance to the east before beginning a more earnest northerly ascent. Enjoy over-the-shoulder views of Lake Hemet and of Garner Valley. Actually, geologists say Garner Valley is not a valley at all but a graben, a long narrow area that down-dropped between two bordering faults.

Garner Graben? Nope, just doesn't have the right ring to it.

The trail climbs steadily into a forest of juniper and Jeffrey and Coulter pine. Most of the time your path is under conifers or the occasional oak. There always seem to be numerous deadfalls to climb over, duck under, or walk around along this stretch of trail.

About a mile from the divide, the going gets steeper and you rapidly gain elevation. Finally you reach the windblown divide just northwest of Spitler Peak and intersect signed Pacific Crest Trail. Enjoy the vistas of forest and desert. Picnic atop one of the divide's many rock outcroppings.

The Pacific Crest Trail, sometimes known as Desert Divide Trail in these parts, offers the energetic a range of options. Heading north on the trail, you soon pass through a section of ghost forest—the charred result of the 1980 Palm Canyon Fire that roared up these slopes from Palm Springs. After ½-mile you'll pass a side trail that

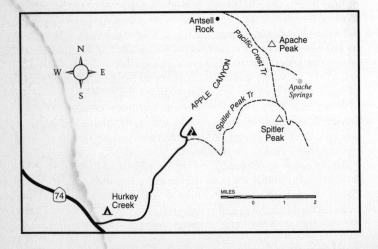

descends steeply another ½-mile to Apache Springs. Another ½-mile along the Pacific Crest Trail brings you to a side trail leading up to bare 7,567-foot Apache Peak.

Another mile brings you to a point just below 7,720-foot Antsell Rock. Unless you're a very good rock climber, stay off the unstable slopes and avoid the urge to ascend to the very top of the rock.

The tram whisks you from palms to pines in just minutes.

Contacting California's Desert Parks and Preserves

Antelope Valley California State Poppy Reserve
1051 West Avenue M
Lancaster, CA 93534
(805) 724–1180

Anza-Borrego Desert State Park
P.O. Box 299
Borrego Springs, CA 92004
(619) 767–5311 or (619) 767–5312

Death Valley National Park
Death Valley, CA 92338
(619) 786–2331

Devil's Punchbowl County Regional Park
28000 Devil's Punchbowl Road
Pearblossom, CA 93553
(805) 944–2743

Joshua Tree National Park
74485 National Park Drive
Twentynine Palms, CA 92277
(619) 367–7511

The Living Desert
47900 Portola Avenue
Palm Desert, CA 92260
(619) 346–5694

Mojave National Preserve
c/o California Desert Information Center
831 Barstow Road
Barstow, CA 92311
(619) 256–8313

Salton Sea National Wildlife Refuge
P.O. Box 120
Calipatria, CA 92233
(619) 348–5278

Salton Sea State Recreation Area
P.O. Box 3166
North Shore, CA 92254
(619) 393–3052 or (619) 393–3059

San Diego County Parks and Recreation
5201 Ruffin Road, Suite P
San Diego, CA 92123
(619) 694–3049

Vasquez Rocks County Park
10700 West Escondido Canyon Road
Saugus, CA 91350
(805) 268–0991

U.S. Bureau of Land Management Offices

Barstow Resource Area
150 Coolwater Lane
Barstow, CA 92311
(619) 255–8700

California Desert District Office
6221 Box Springs Boulevard
Riverside, CA 92507
(909) 697–5200

El Centro Resource Area
1661 South Fourth Street
El Centro, CA 92243
(619) 357–4400

Needles Resource Area
101 West Spikes Road
Needles, CA 92363
(619) 326–3896

Palm Springs Resource Area
63–500 Garnet Avenue
North Palm Springs, CA 92258
(619) 251–4800

Ridgecrest Resource Area
300 South Richmond Road
Ridgecrest, CA 92363
(619) 384–5400

Index